A nostalgic look at
LIVERPOOL
TRAMS
1945-1957

Steve Palmer & Brian Martin

Silver Link Publishing Ltd

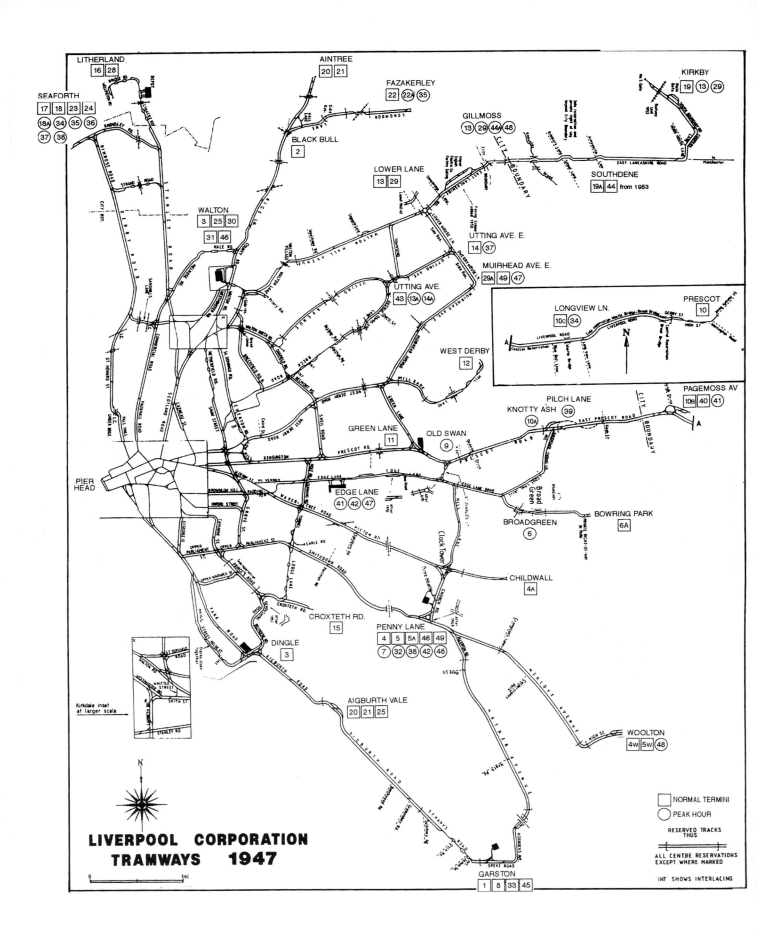

CONTENTS

Title page Standing proudly in front of Baby Grand 279 is Walter Benstead, with 36 years' service and soon to retire with the last trams. Photographed during the last summer of tram operation at Castle Street loop, on a hospital special. *Brian Martin*

Above A busy scene at Islington Square in April 1954, with Baby Grands 205 and 242 on route 29A to and from Muirhead Avenue, and some now vintage cars! *Richard Wiseman*

© Steve Palmer and Brian Martin 1996

All rights reserved. No part of this publication may be reproduced, stored in a retrieval system or transmitted, in any form or by any means, electronic, mechanical, photocopying, recording or otherwise, without prior permission in writing from Silver Link Publishing Ltd.

First published in October 1996

British Library Cataloguing in Publication Data

A catalogue record for this book is available from the British Library.

ISBN 1 85794 059 8

Silver Link Publishing Ltd
Unit 5, Home Farm Close
Church Street, Wadenhoe
Peterborough PE8 5TE
Tel (01832) 720440
Fax (01832) 720531
e-mail: pete@slinkp-p.demon.co.uk

Printed and bound in Great Britain

ACKNOWLEDGEMENTS

IN WORKING together on preparing this book on the fine Liverpool tramway, we have both enjoyed recalling those happy years riding on the trams. We would like to acknowledge the support of many people who supplied illustrations, maps and information, which complete this interesting and nostalgic record of the post-war tramway years.

Our thanks go to Martin Jenkins, whose vast collection was made available and from which we were able to choose many illustrations, including the colour views taken by him towards the end of the tramway and which enhance the jacket and colour pages. He was a local enthusiast who followed tramway events with his camera until the system's demise in 1957. Today he fulfils his interests in tramways by compiling and commentating on the Online Videos - including one on Liverpool Tramways and others to follow.

We also express our appreciation to T. B. Maund and J. B. Horne for allowing us to reproduce maps of the city from their distinguished series on Liverpool Transport. The assistance of Peter Rogan in helping to contact Ken Dodd for the Foreword, J. W. Gahan for information and Steve Molloy for map-scanning is also acknowledged. In particular we thank Terry Daniel for his skill in drawing five maps of the city areas, complete with the complicated track layout and depots; J. H. Price was also helpful in loaning a useful system map from his collection.

Amongst the more than 300 illustrations in this book are some taken by the authors, and many from other enthusiasts, to whom we express our appreciation: Richard Wiseman, Robert Fergusson, Michael Harrison and David Packer, also E. A. Gahan, K. G. Harvie, the late J. H. Roberts, F. Lloyd Jones and R. F. Mack, together with the Merseyside Tramway Preservation Society.

We also wish to acknowledge the professional assistance of Glynn Wilton of the National Tramway Museum, who has produced the fascinating prints of the skilled photographer H. B. Priestley, whose Liverpool photographs contribute to the quality of this book. The photographs of the late R. B. Parr and N. N. Forbes are also in the historic collection of the National Tramway Museum, whose permission was given for them to be reproduced here. Consequently the photographer's names have been credited, together with the initials 'NTM' to identify the National Tramway Museum.

Finally we thank the City of Liverpool for allowing the use of their famous coat of arms, which was carried by the trams throughout their life.

BIBLIOGRAPHY

Blackburn, R. E. *Liverpool Tramways 1943-1957* (LRTA)

Cormack, I. L. *Green Goddesses Go East* (STMS)

Horne, J. B., and Maund, T. B. *Liverpool Transport*, Vol 1 19th Century, Vol 2 1900-1930, Vol 3 1931-1939, Vol 4 1939-1957, Vol 5 1957-1986 (TPC)

Martin, B. P. *Edge Lane Roundabout* (MTPS)

Martin, T. J. *Liverpool Trams Fleet List* (MTPS) *Liverpool Corporation Tramways 1937-1957*, Parts 1, 2 and 3 (MTPS)

Vaughan, Eric *By Tram To Garston* (MTPS)

FOREWORD

Ken Dodd OBE

HOW TICKLED I WAS to be asked to write the foreword for a book on the dear old Liverpool Green Goddesses. In fact it is quite tattifalarious!

Where I grew up and still live, the trams used to pass our family home - just down the road was the famous Knotty Ash tram terminus. In fact just nearby were the equally famous Jam Butty Mines. Quite a lot of my little friends - the Diddymen - used to work there and get the tram home.

Seriously though, the trams were part of my life - they were there in the street, and part of life; nobody had motor cars, everybody went by tram. We knew most of the tram drivers by name and quite often on my journeys down to Old Swan I'd be allowed to stand by the driver and wave to all my friends on the way.

My dad and uncle were coal merchants in the area and because my uncle was so small I suppose he became the inspiration for the Diddymen. I suppose his character just grew and grew!

I remember the trams as they passed Springfield Park and swept round the curve by the brush works and the village hall to the tram stop by Mother's Pantry. It was here one day I was accosted by a fellow passenger.

'Will I get a shock', she asked, 'if I put my foot on the tram lines?'

'Only if you put the other one on the overhead wires, then we'd all get a shock!' said I, brandishing my tickling stick.

Since those days, keeping up the legends of Knotty Ash and the Jam Butty Mines has always reminded me of those happy days of my childhood. The collection of photographs in the book brings it all back. Liverpool in the 1940s and '50s certainly was a golden age when everyone was glad to be home from the war - to get back to the city and be welcomed by the familiar sight of a Green Goddess to take them home. In the pictures so much was destroyed by wartime, and equally as much was demolished in the slum clearance schemes of the '60s. The pages that follow show so much of the Liverpool that was.

Some of the childhood memories of the trams obviously include the celebrated penny returns - where a kid could, in the school holidays, go all the way there and back for just one penny! Many a kid was kept off the street corners by exploring the many country areas that were reached by the trams - Woolton, Prescot, Kirkby, Aintree and Bowring Park. Who remembers getting the 4W tram to Woolton to visit Jackson's Farm to fish for 'jackies'?

One unforgettable memory is of the flower 'girls' going home from their pitches at Clayton Square, piling high their baskets on the open front platforms of the trams, just barely leaving room for the driver.

How wonderful it was too when the illuminated tram visited our route. It was a splendid sight to see with the tramways band playing on the open top - it certainly brightened up the city. Pity the war put paid to it.

Many a son of this great seaport was glad to see the trams when they came on leave. Some were glad to get back too! An old grizzled seafarer off back to the China Seas travelled to the docks to pick up his ship on one of the old open-top trams and bounced all the way. On alighting he was heard to mutter, 'Well, that's the worst part of the voyage over!'

Of course Liverpool was always snobbish concerning its trams - we even had First Class trams, posh inside with velvet cushions and curtains, but very spartan for the workers on the top deck! Even our location at Knotty Ash had a choice of two routes from town. The posh way was on the 40 via the greenery of Broadgreen instead of the rows of shops of Prescot Road on the 10B route.

I certainly was discumknockerated when they replaced the trams with characterless buses. First they began whittling down the Prescot Road trams until the friendly 10B passed Knotty Ash for the last time. Thankfully we still had the 40 passing our house until the very last day of the trams - 14 September 1957.

6   LIVERPOOL TRAMS 1945-1957

AUTHORS' INTRODUCTION

I REMEMBER CLEARLY Liverpool's tramway system and the characteristics of the Green Goddesses in the City Centre and standing in circulars at Pier Head! Riding on the trams was slower in the busy central area, as convoys of trams and buses proceeded via Dale Street and Church Street respectively. However, I also recall travelling to Liverpool by Ribble X61 coach and, on reaching Scotland Road, seeing a tram on route 44 - from Walton Road - swinging along in front of us with its trolley rope swaying behind, much to the annoyance of our coach driver! In the city centre I remember seeing a burning Marks car being shunted into South Castle Street, and at Pier Head in 1947 finding out that a Green Lane Depot fire had destroyed many trams. I demanded from my parents that I rode on the 10B tram to see it - and remember it to this day!

In 1956 I remember riding to Kirkby at speed along the light rail line parallel to the East Lancashire Road, and subsequently travelling by bus to see the 31 Streamliners hidden on a siding prior to scrapping. Finally, on the last day - 14 September 1957 - travelling to Liverpool with a special ticket on tram J (213), an epic ride in the procession to Bowring Park and back to Edge Lane Depot. Standing in the crowd and watching Liverpool's last tram disappearing into the Works was a very moving experience. I have never forgotten it, and therefore found the experience of writing and compiling this 'Nostalgic look at Liverpool Trams' a rewarding task, commemorating in retrospect the finest tramway, and hoping for the future.

Steve Palmer

I HAVE BEEN in love with the trams of my home city since I was a schoolboy of eight. The first seeds were sown watching Green Goddesses miraculously changing the electric points, the trolley always taking the right direction, and seeing indicators being turned, always wanting to find out the next, half-hidden destination. The trams absolutely fascinated me - I wanted to know all there was about them.

The spell had been cast by those lumbering green monsters that passed our house in Edge Lane. As I became interested it was obvious that the trams were being phased out and, joining with other enthusiasts, life became one round after another of last trams, culminating of course in the closure of my own routes, the 6A and 40, when the last tram disappeared from view on 14 September 1957. A very sad and sombre day indeed.

But we all believed that trams had the right attributes and were cast aside only because of post-war lack of cash. The qualities were obvious to all thinking people, and today those qualities are ensuring a rediscovery of the tramcar. Manchester and Sheffield have brought trams back. They are quiet, smooth, comfortable and environmentally friendly, and amazingly they are now being described as flexible! Suddenly they are back in fashion.

In this book we have tried to rekindle memories of Liverpool's tram days - those everlasting summer days on a tram ride to Bowring Park with the driver's door open with the smell of new-mown grass mingling with the scents of hot electricity and the 'clutch, clutch' sounds from the contactor cupboard. Or perhaps a high-speed run on a bogie car. Yes, Liverpool's trams were the fastest - and the best-loved!

Brian Martin

Above left A nostalgic view of Streamliner 942 in Roe Street, outside St George's Hall and the Royal Court Theatre, during an LRTL tour on 1 June 1952. On this occasion the tour travelled many tramway miles for enthusiasts: Kirkby, Walton, Longview Lane, Bowring Park, Garston and Mather Avenue. You will notice that the trolley is 'angle-working', and its rope is framing the Queen Square sign, long since demolished and now the site of a busy street of buses. *Richard Wiseman*

Left Fazakerley tram terminus with Streamliner 950 on a summer day in 1947, surrounded by the trees and a hedge in the foreground. 'TURN LEFT' says the sign for traffic, to avoid ending in the field outside the City boundary! *R. B. Parr, NTM*

Right A familiar scene in 1957 in Elliot Street, with old St John's Market, at the spot where now exists a flight of steps to Great Charlotte Street. In the background can be seen the former Owen Owen building. *Brian Martin*

A BRIEF HISTORICAL BACKGROUND TO THE POST-WAR LIVERPOOL TRAMWAY

IT IS FOUR DECADES since the last Liverpool tram finally left the Pier Head to the cacophony of ships' sirens, hooters and the band of the LCPT, and the famous Green Goddess trams departed for ever. Undoubtedly this event deprived Liverpool of a famous part of its scene, which today, with the return of modern trams to Manchester and Sheffield, is being shown to have been its best form of transport. How had Liverpool qualified as the finest

city tramway in this country, on many grounds, since 1897?

In 1943, with the extension of the tramway to Kirkby, there were 97 miles of routes, 63 tram services and 744 trams. Of these significant factors, it is worth recording that 27.88 miles of the tram routes were on reservation in the suburbs, starting with the extension of the Edge Lane route to Bowring Park in 1914. Following the First World War the City Engineer, J. A. Brodie, designed these dual carriageway centre reservations leading through the newly developed suburbs of the 1920s, an example that

Left **St Nicholas Place in the early years of the century, showing the parish church and the bridges of the Overhead Railway, together with the terminus of the trams.** *National Tramway Museum collection*

Below left **An aerial view of the Pier Head in 1930, showing the three loops for the many tram routes: North Loop (left) via St Nicholas Place, Centre Loop via Water Street and South Loop via Brunswick Street. This is clearly a busy tram terminus, and there are very few buses.** *Liverpool City Engineers, NTM*

Below **A striking view from the 1920s, looking down Lime Street with St George's Hall, Walker Art Gallery and the Duke of Wellington column dominating the scene. In addition to service trams can be seen one in St George's Place - on route 28 Litherland - and a Ribble bus, together with many robust taxis.** *National Tramway Museum collection*

Left This is Standard 772 - built at Edge Lane Works - in September 1933, with the new 1930s green and cream livery with flares that resulted in the trams being christened 'Green Goddesses'. *National Tramway Museum collection*

Right The first LRTL (Light Railway Transport League) tour on the new trams, using 894, on 14 May 1939, is seen here in St John's Lane, in front of Lime Street station, with another tram in service on route 24. Amongst the crowd of enthusiasts can be seen General Manager Walter Marks, seen in his suit and homburg hat, who accompanied them on the tour of the whole system: Prescot to Allerton to Seaforth and the East Lancashire Road. *R. B. Parr, NTM collection*

Below Car 868 - the first of the bogie Streamliners - pictured in June 1936 turning into Menlove Avenue after a trip to Woolton, on a first trial journey. *National Tramway Museum collection*

offered inspiration to other cities. Examples of such locations depicted in this book are Aigburth Road in 1921, Fazakerley and Muirhead Avenue in 1923, Woolton, Mather Avenue, Townsend Avenue and Utting Avenue in 1924, Walton Hall Avenue to Stopgate Lane in 1925, and Allerton Station to Long Lane in 1928. Thus in all areas of the city the tramway operated where the sleepered track was grassed over and enclosed from the roads by neat and attractive privet hedges. Residents of the suburbs - many of them on council estates - could board the 'light rail' trams and travel freely and at speed on the modern cars towards their workplaces and the city centre.

Many other dual carriageways were also built with potential tramway reservation - like Queens Drive - and in 1935, after a gap of seven years, the extensions were completed! Reservation was further extended to Childwall in 1936, Edge Lane Drive for route 40 in 1937, Muirhead Avenue East in 1938 and Allerton to Garston in 1939. The East Lancashire Road was extended in stages: to Lower House Lane in 1938, Stonebridge Lane in 1940, Gillmoss in 1941 and Kirkby in 1943, serving the ordnance factory there. This took the tramway outside the City boundary and was built under the Powers (Defence) Act of 1939, together with the links along Dwerryhouse Lane and Lower House Lane, which were also completed in 1943. Thus the Liverpool tramway system reached its maximum size.

In the post-war years there were plans for the extension of tramway routes - from Garston to Speke, Croxteth Road along Ullet Road, Muirhead Avenue to Page Moss across country, from Utting Avenue East to Carr Lane, and

a new depot at Stonebridge Lane. The latter was needed because 82 trams had to be stored in the open, since the seven existing depots accommodated only 662 trams!

The new class of trams in the '30s were built by LCPT at Edge Lane Works from 1931. This classic building - complete with central traverser for moving trams to different departments - had opened in 1928. The new construction commenced with Standards 758-769, and the first cars in the olive-green and cream livery, 770-781, followed by Robinson Cabin cars 782-817 of 1934, Marks cars 818-867 of 1935-6, culminating in the bogie Streamliners. These were designed by R. J. Heathman, who had been appointed as Engineering Draughtsman in 1935, coming from the English Electric factory at Preston where he had been involved in designing the Blackpool Streamliners. This new generation of 263 attractive, modern cars comprised 163 bogie Streamliners (151-199 and 868-992) and 100 four-wheelers (201-300) known as Baby Grands. The olive-green and cream liveried trams also appeared in the 1930s and gained the nickname 'Green Goddesses' from the popular film of the period starring George Arliss. It contrasted with the previous crimson lake and ivory fleet livery.

Of the 744 trams that existed in 1945, 390 were four-wheeled old-type cars and 354 were the modern cars built at Edge Lane Works in the '30s. Consequently the trams outnumbered buses by a ratio of three to one, yet the older trams needed replacing by proposed new trams, designed by R. J. Heathman towards the end of the war. Interestingly, these drawings showed them to have centre

Edge Lane Works, flying its flag on the last day of tramway operation - 14 September 1957 - with a service tram and a new bus stop sign - a very sad scene! *Brian Martin*

entrances - similar to Blackpool - together with PCC equipment and bogies.

After the war the General Manager, Walter Marks, prepared plans for the development of public transport in Liverpool. It is very interesting to recall his long-term alternatives: diesel buses, trolleybuses and an enlarged light rail system on reserved track, including 38 miles of street track transferring to reservation by road widening. There was also a proposal for the inclusion of modern American-type PCC cars, 48 feet in length, double-ended with centre exits, which would necessitate the enlarging of the depots. It was proposed that English Electric should construct the PCC cars for Liverpool, and other cities were involved, including Blackpool, Leeds, Sheffield and Glasgow. The costs of these three post-war schemes were £3.7 million for the buses, £4.4 million for the trolleybuses - with extensive overhead - and £6.7 million for the improved tramway with new Liverpool bogie double-deckers. This showed the contrast in their respective costs; and if the PCC trams were introduced to replace the existing trams, this would cost £7.4 million! However, Marks's report did not seem to include the compromise of regional development of some tram routes and replacement of others by buses. Thus it would appear that the 28 miles of credible reservation could have been retained and extended beyond the terminus to new areas, and

inwards towards the city centre, while some areas of entire street track - like Bootle - could have been converted to buses, still leaving a significant tramway network for the city.

The alternatives were considered by the Passenger Transport Committee on 16 October 1945, and they decided to choose the cheapest alternative of buses. In November that year - following the local elections - Councillor G. W. G. Armour, Transport Chairman, claimed that the continued presence of the tramway would greatly hamper the creation of Liverpool's new roads.

Consequently the Council accepted the scrapping of the Liverpool tramway, and a plan was devised by 1947 comprising several annual stages from 1948 to 1958. In retrospect, when one considers the demise of a fine tramway in relation to the current volume of city transport, with its competing buses and pollution, it indicates failure! By contrast is the success of the Manchester light rail system, which has trams operating through the city centre from Bury and Altrincham, together with the opening of a new Sheffield city tramway. Happily consideration is now being given to the reintroduction of modern trams in Liverpool - relating to the Marks scheme of 1944. Some familiar destinations - like Page Moss - have been mentioned, and headlines in the local press give encouragement: RETURN OF THE TRAMS - TRAMS ON WAY BACK - TRAMS MAY ROLL AGAIN.

Hold tight! We hope to be able to enjoy tram riding in Liverpool again - cleaner, smoother and more comfortable - by the Millennium!

THE CITY CENTRE

Right Passing the Town Hall at the corner of Castle Street on 11 August 1955, Streamliner 992 - the highest numbered of Liverpool's trams - has already changed its indicator for the return journey before arriving at Pier Head. The tram is followed by a Morris Oxford, a Ford Prefect and a bus on route 18D. The pedestrians using the crossing are passing railway signs showing - in opposite directions - Exchange station in Tithebarn Street and Central station in Ranelagh Street. Today the trains travel underground between them, but the stations themselves have disappeared in property development. *R. B. Parr, NTM*

Left and below This striking view shows Baby Grand 241 leaving Pier Head on route 6A to Bowring Park, and is dominated by the impressive Liver Building. In 1957 - the last year of tramway operation - the Liver Building presents a rather macabre appearance, covered with a coating of soot from the visiting ships over many years. Subsequently it was cleaned, and today looks decidedly distinguished above the landscaped gardens at this location. As the tram leaves the South Loop it passes the Cunard Building, while the large number of buses in the background shows that this is approaching the Tramway Finale in September. However, the Liver Birds remain perched high above the terminus today. The 1996 view also shows the statue of King Edward VII, now in the centre of a pedestrian boulevard complete with trees and seats. But perhaps it rather lacks the former character of the terminal loops for the trams and buses? *J. W. Martin/Steve Palmer*

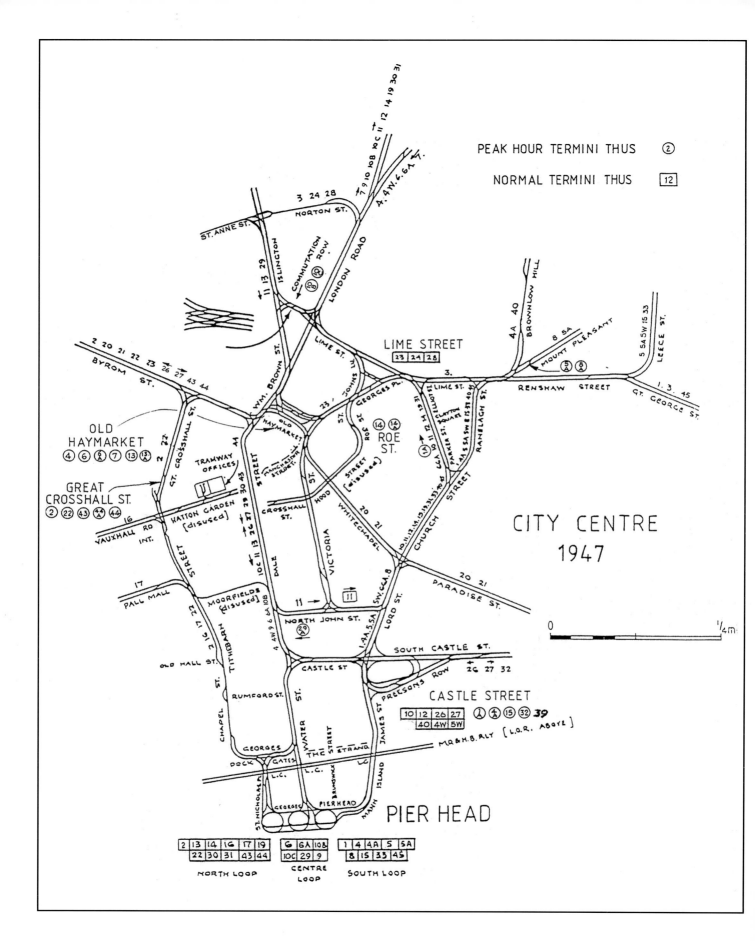

LIVERPOOL TRAMS 1945-1957

Meeting the ships

Above In 1947 the Pier Head terminus featured three loops for 30 routes, providing a unique city centre terminus serving the ferries' George's Landing Stage. Workers arriving from Birkenhead, Seacombe and New Brighton could board trams to all parts of the city.

Looking out from the Mersey Docks & Harbour Board Building, here is a splendid view of the Pier Head, with the Canadian Pacific liner *Empress of Canada* being towed into the Prince's Landing Stage by tugs. Being a Sunday, few buses and only two trams can be seen on the South Loop, while the statue of King Edward VII dominates. Zebra crossings now help the pedestrians reach the tramway terminus, while a Green Goddess tram leaves for Kirkby on route 19. *Valentine's, Dundee*

Right A picturesque view from the Liver Building showing trams on the North Loop, which served the northern routes of Seaforth, Litherland, Aintree, Fazakerley and East Lancashire Road. Here we can see trams of several types, including Robinson Cabin Cars and Streamliners, which compare interestingly from this height. The floating landing stage served the ferries, and *Wallasey* approaches from Birkenhead, while the Isle of Man Steam Packet Company ship *Monas Queen* is at the Prince's Landing Stage. This was a daily

service to Douglas and at peak holiday times, in July and August, extra boats are brought into service. Trams waiting on the Pier Head loops was a familiar sight to ships' passengers. *Martin Jenkins*

The Mersey Docks & Harbour Board Building at Pier Head makes an impressive background for the trams approaching the South Loop on 30 May 1955. All the Green Goddess trams are a striking sight - Baby Grand 202 on route 13 via Dale Street can be seen giving way to Streamliner 183 on route 14 via Church Street. Trams on 6A and 40 are waiting on the approach line having unloaded; previously - in 1947 - the Page Moss route 40 terminated in South Castle Street. By the summer of 1955 the remaining routes 13 and 14, 19 and 44, 6A and 40 were maintaining the presence of trams at Pier Head, while a bus on route 87 replaced trams to Garston on the 8 and 33 routes in June 1953. *H. B. Priestley, NTM*

Green Goddess trams on the South Loop in April 1954, with the mounted figure of King Edward VII in its centre. The trams are on routes 40, 19, 10B, 14 and 44, and a girl boards 953, the nearest one. As the trams approach the loop line, an inspector designates their location according to their time of departure. Trams leave in turn, and the passengers - having chosen their destination - enjoy circling the loop. Certainly this was a famous terminus for the Green Goddess trams. 'Relieve the pain' recommends 953! *H. B. Priestley, NTM*

At Pier Head on 26 August 1953 Streamliner 169 turns out of the Centre Loop on route 29 for Muirhead Avenue East. Before turning into Water Street, the driver waits for the crossing pedestrians. Fortunately the L-driver of an Austin car has left the pedestrian crossing behind! The south-west building of the Prince's Dock and other warehouses at the quayside used by the liners can be seen. By 1953 the North Loop was used by buses only, while eight tram routes were still in service from Pier Head. The pattern of the tramway's overhead and span wires is like a giant cobweb in the sky. *H. B. Priestley, NTM*

Leaving Pier Head via Mann Island in the summer of 1957, Baby Grand 299, heading for Page Moss, first passes under the Overhead Railway bridge, abandoned in 1956. Notice that the trolley has swung to the left of the tram because of the low level of the bridge. The traffic in James Street is light on this Sunday afternoon, and we can see the new St George's Crescent, built in the 1950s. At the corner is a handsome red and white building, designed in 1898 for the Pacific Steam Navigation Company. At the foot of the corner of the wall can be seen the letters 'EWS' - emergency water supply - a wartime survival. The road still has stone sets, while today they are covered with tarmac, busy with traffic controlled by traffic lights - and no trams! *Brian Martin*

Above A handsome scene in Derby Square on 14 April 1955, as a convoy of trams on routes 40, 19 and 6A moves up James Street, passing the commercial buildings including the First National Bank. The Midland Bank is today the Trials Hotel. An Austin van races Baby Grand 251 to enter Lord Street first! The tram track had been relaid here by 1953 to remove the junction with Castle Street, whose tram services had been converted to buses. Note how clear was the trams' route indicator number, helpful to passengers in the city centre. Note also the temporary stop bollard in the left foreground. *R. B. Parr, NTM*

Left The magnificent statue of Queen Victoria beneath its dome and protected during the war in a bomb-damaged area, forms the centre of a turning loop for routes 10, 12, 26, 27 and 40. Standard 13 is seen in South Castle Street turning into Preesons Row on service 12 to West Derby, with the Town Hall in the background, on 9 May 1947. Here is located a small office for the duty Inspector, where the staff could have a break. The tram is smartly repainted with the 'Liverpool Corporation Passenger Transport' lettering without the coat of arms. *A. C. Noon*

Left On Easter Sunday 1996 it is a deserted scene, but all the buildings and the monument are intact, although now surrounded by a pedestrian precinct where the trams used to terminate. Behind the photographer is the new Queen Elizabeth II Law Courts building, which enclosed South Castle Street in 1983-84. *Steve Palmer*

LIVERPOOL TRAMS 1945-1957

Above A very festive view of Lord Street, dressed for the Coronation in June 1953, with 'E II R' banners hanging from the lighting poles. The public transport is certainly disciplined by the trams, with buses following the trams in line. Baby Grand 245 - the one surviving in Liverpool today - on route 40 is heading for Page Moss, while a Streamliner approaches on route 33 from Garston, led by a taxi. On the corner of Paradise Street and Lord Street is the famous Bunney's department store. This view of the trams in service must precede the closing of routes 8 and 33 on 6 June 1953, following Coronation Day. Today part of Lord Street is a pedestrian precinct without trams and traffic. *Brian Martin collection*

Streamliner 966 on route 40 outside the famous Owen Owen store in Clayton Square on 14 April 1955. Behind the following tram on route 14 the building under construction became Littlewoods' Spinney House. There is a very neat lamp on the tram stop pole, and the pedestrians look smartly turned out for the shopping centre. Today this street is also a pedestrian precinct without trams and traffic, while Owen Owen was closed and became a supermarket in 1994. *R. B. Parr, NTM*

Central and Lime Street stations

Clayton Square looking towards Church Street in July 1947, showing Streamliner 951 on route 1 to Garston loading from the tram stop island. Note again the rather elegant standard lamps, originally gas lamps, with cross-arms used by the lamplighter's ladder. At this time pedestrians are able to stroll across the roads, there being not very much traffic - there is an elegantly dressed lady in the foreground. Wills's Capstan cigarettes dominate the scene, with the roof of Lime Street station behind. *H. B. Priestley, NTM*

A nostalgic view along Ranelagh Street, with just one tram to be seen passing Central station on 14 September 1957, on its way to Pier Head; after this date the trams will not be seen here again. While this is a busy shopping street with a variety of shops - including the large Lewis's building - the scene is dominated by the Adelphi Hotel, at the corner of Lime Street and Brownlow Hill. Where the pedestrians are crossing the tramlines in the foreground, it can clearly be seen that the trams have been made one-way here. *M. Harrison*

LIVERPOOL TRAMS 1945-1957

Right Baby Grand 216 passes the imposing facade and forecourt of Liverpool
Central station on a quiet Sunday. The
station is advertising fares to Sheffield,
Doncaster, Rotherham and Hull. At the
junction of Church Street and Ranelagh
Street, today the station is underground
for local trains. *Brian Martin*

Below right On Easter Sunday 1996 a
police car is on duty in place of the tram,
and a modern-looking shopping centre
was built in place of Central station early
in 1977. Apart from this, Ranelagh Street
looks very familiar, with Lewis's and the
Adelphi Hotel looking very clean! The
paving on which the police car stands
indicates that this is the entrance to a
pedestrian shopping precinct in Church
Street and Parker Street. *Steve Palmer*

Below A view from St John's Lane,
showing a Green Goddess Liner passing
Lime Street station on 11 September
1955. While the station is still in position
today, the Royal Hotel has been demolished and in the 1960s there was a reconstruction of the forecourt with a pedestrian precinct. Today there is much traffic at
this point - with convoys of buses - and
the local railway loop is underground.
Undoubtedly this 1955 scene is enhanced
by the tram travelling along Lime Street.
Martin Jenkins

The Overhead Railway

A very interesting view from the roof of the Liver Building in 1948, looking into Water Street and showing three modes of rail transport: the Liverpool Overhead Railway and beneath it a Mersey Docks & Harbour Board steam locomotive, while Streamliner 904 waits to proceed. The Overhead Railway - opened in 1893 - operated between Seaforth and Dingle, serving the dock workers and providing a fascinating journey for the public! Sadly it was closed on 30 December 1956, considerable expense being anticipated for the restoration of the overhead structure. In that year both trams and the Overhead Railway disappeared from this scene.
G. W. Price

A striking view in Water Street, with the Overhead Railway passing over Baby Grand 203, followed by an AEC bus bound for Hunts Cross on route 72. Tram route 6A to Bowring Park was one of thirteen routes that traversed the city centre via Dale Street, as shown it on their nearside indicator. The Cunard Building is seen behind the tram, while the Overhead Railway carries on advert for a well-known product, Barker & Dobson's chocolate. On the pavement on the right is a police telephone next to the 'Cars Stop' sign, while the striped duty box is for a policeman on traffic duty. Look out for the manhole cover lifted on the left!
Brian Martin collection

LIVERPOOL TRAMS 1945-1957

DALE STREET

Right This is Dale Street, at the corner of Castle Street, and Streamliner 984 on route 44 and AEC bus A716 wait for pedestrians to cross in August 1955. Interesting points include the large Austin car turning the corner, the feeder cable to the overhead and Reece & Sons dairy and confectionery shop for city workers! *R. B. Parr, NTM*

Below right Baby Grand 208 on route 44 from Southdene to Pier Head traverses Dale Street in 1956, with the handsome Municipal Buildings of 1866 dominating the scene. There are many commercial buildings, with shops providing a variety of services to the office workers; the elegant tram stop stands outside 'Fags Ltd'. Today there are sandwich shops along Dale Street for the workers, and all the traffic is one-way towards Pier Head. There are many competing buses of different companies, but sadly no trams on the ten city routes as in post-war years. *Brian Martin*

Below At the top of Dale Street Robinson Cabin Car 796 on route 13 is bound for Pier Head on 22 April 1952. The tram track junction in the foreground is with Byrom Street, where nine routes joined from the north of the city, Aintree, Fazakerley and Bootle. Cars are parked adjacent to the Mersey Tunnel, and the boys are walking past a Jowett Javelin saloon car. Compared with the cobbled street, the newly laid tram track is enhanced by the smooth surface of the tarmac! Note the man working on top of the tower wagon on the left, possibly cleaning the lamp shades; these enhance the entrance to Queensway, opened by King George V in July 1934. *H. B. Priestley, NTM*

LIVERPOOL TRAMS 1945-1957

OLD HAYMARKET

Left The Old Haymarket siding for peak-hour trams is seen here on 10 April 1954. Streamliner 166 stands at the stop, while the passengers board and the crew stand talking at the front. In the foreground are the double crossovers, which enabled trams to be located for their loading positions. Facing the tram is the distinctive Technical College building at the corner of William Brown Street and Byrom Street. Note the coat of arms in the centre, and the elaborate carvings in the triangular pediments. The buses are advertising Mackeson's and Dulux. *H. B. Priestley, NTM*

Below left Car 219 is on route 13 to Lower Lane at its peak-hour terminus at Old Haymarket. The conductor in his smart uniform wears the fast Ultimate ticket machine, and waits for the passengers. In the background Liner 916 passes the Liverpool City Museum in William Brown Street on its way down to Pier Head via Dale Street, but while the trams have been smartened by being repainted in 1955, the museum needs cleaning to remove the smoke deposits of many years. Today the buildings are clean, but the trams had departed from this location by 5 November 1955. *R. B. Parr, NTM*

Top right Streamliner 950 passes the Liverpool City Museum in William Brown Street on 4 April 1953 followed by a Royal Mail Commer van. The trolley has passed under the skate in the overhead, which turns the points into Islington for route 13 trams, but 6A will continue up towards London Road. *R. B. Parr, NTM*

Middle right The Duke of Wellington column dominates the scene as two peak-hour Baby Grands on route 14, 204 and 239, pass at the junction of Islington and London Road near Old Haymarket in August 1955. A policeman controls the traffic and the sky is patterned by the tramway overhead at the junction; note the drop-arm that re-sets the frog when the trolley of each tram hits it. Along Commutation Row, Burton's marble frontage enhances the scene, but is rivalled by the nearby 'Player's Please'! The cyclist must be feeling the effect of the cobbles as he follows the tram, unless he rides on the tarmac between the tram rails. *R. B. Parr, NTM*

Right At Easter 1996 all the buildings and the column are intact, although since 1990 William Brown Street has provided parking for visitors to the Liverpool Museum and the Walker Art Gallery. *Steve Palmer*

Above An interesting view of the entrance of the Queensway Mersey Tunnel in 1947, with a number of busy trams heading for Pier Head via William Brown Street and joining the queue in Dale Street. The trams look rather grubby at this stage, notably the Green Goddess Liner on route 11, which is in the pre-war style with a 'white' roof. On the right a tram is seen turning into Byrom Street, which the nine northern routes use along Scotland Road. The rather decorative street lighting columns can again be seen in the foreground, together with the elegant column opposite the Queensway entrance. Costing £8 million, the tunnel was opened by King George V on 18 July 1934, and was named after Queen Mary. On the left is the striking sign for Hessy's, advertising 'Musical Instruments and Radio'. *Commercial photograph*

Left The same location at Easter 1996 shows again the parked cars in William Brown Street, where the trams used to run, the distinct entrance to the Mersey Tunnel and the flyover that has brought Churchill Way into Dale Street since the 1970s. *Steve Palmer*

St George's Hall

Above On 5 June 1954 we see the elegant facade of St George's Hall, with Liner 179 turning from Lime Street into London Road, on its way to Walton Depot after the rush hour. A policeman controls the traffic, made conspicuous by his white coat and gloves and standing in a striped box! The shelter for tram passengers is noticeable on the island, with traffic passing behind it. While St George's Hall's Classical facade - built in 1838 - has been turned black by the sooty atmosphere in those days. Today it is much cleaner and looks handsome! *Richard Wiseman*

Below Car 577 stands in Roe Street, the terminus of the 14 and 14A, in 1947, dominated by the imposing end of St George's Hall with its beautiful sculptured pediment. The facade of the North Western Hotel is seen in the background, which today is part of the Liverpool John Moores University. Both trams are seen unvestibuled and in the earlier livery of maroon and cream. Passengers are waiting at the tram stop for the next car. *N. N. Forbes, NTM*

A view from Commutation Row on 21 April 1954, as a Green Goddess Liner on route 13 passes Rushworth & Dreaper's musical stores on Islington. The points in the foreground are by now disused and only kept for emergency use. A Morris Oxford leads the traffic in the foreground. Men on their ladders are painting the sign for theatre tickets, serving the famous Empire, Royal Court and Playhouse theatres and the Pavilion in Lodge Lane. *H. B. Priestley*

LONDON ROAD

Streamliner 187 turns from Moss Street into London Road on route 19 from Kirkby to Pier Head. The policeman guards the crossing from the platform in the centre of the junction, marked by the striped pole. Today, to the right-hand side is the Royal Liverpool Hospital, but in August 1955 there was the Majestic Cinema at the corner of Boundary Street and Daulby Street. In this interesting scene a van waits for the tram to turn the corner, and there is a police phone box on the corner - handy for the café! *R. B. Parr, NTM*

BROWNLOW HILL

In August 1957 - the last season for the trams - Baby Grand 296 is seen in Brownlow Hill, heading for Clayton Square on a Sunday. It approaches the single track section at the side of the Adelphi Hotel - a space for parked limousines! At the corner of Bamford Street the tram passes Milligan's Government Surplus Stores. It is interesting to look along the street and realise that all the buildings have gone today; in the distance 'Beer - the Best Long Drink in the World' is being advertised. If you look at the overhead, you will see a contactor skate, which operated the single-line signal. The Morris Minor passing the tram is being driven by a learner with the British School of Motoring. *R. B. Parr, NTM*

THE OUTER CIRCULAR AND CROSS-CITY ROUTES

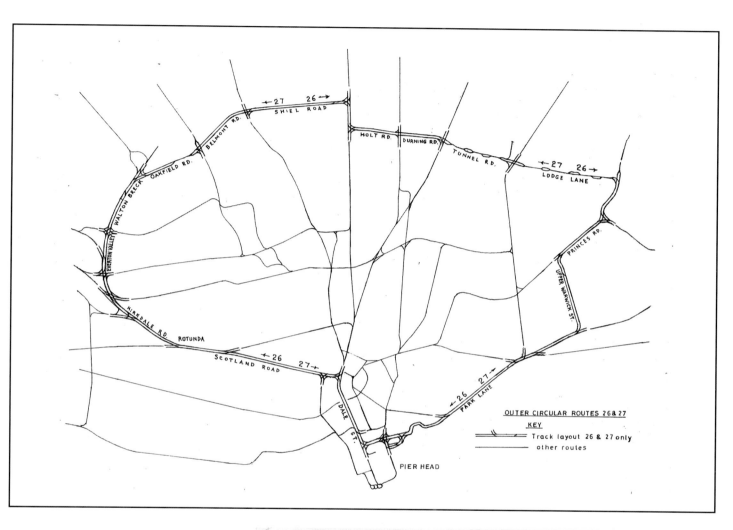

A busy scene in South Castle Street in 1947, with several trams on the 26 and 27 Outer Circular route and two trams on the 12 West Derby route, which are circling the Victoria monument. Priestly bogie-car 776 - the first series to carry the 'Green Goddess' livery in 1933 - is looking smarter than the more modern Streamliners seen here! The Marks car 852 carries the pre-war red route number 26, while 776 has the new white-on-black 26. A new brick wall can be seen on the right enclosing a bombed site, while the elegant Mersey Tunnel ventilator shaft on the right contrasts with the cast-iron facade of a building in Harrington Street on the left! *F. N. T. Lloyd Jones*

Priestly bogie car 781, one of four in the series with a shallow domed roof, heads outwards along Dale Street. The distinctive Blackburn Assurance building survives today, but the buildings on the right were demolished in the 1970s to make way for the Churchill Way flyover, which reaches ground level here today. The buildings ahead were the famous city centre department store Unity House, the Co-op's flagship premises in Liverpool. Note the distinctive pair of eyes on each side of the tram's route indicator - advertising *Picture Post* every Wednesday! Two young boys watch the passengers board the tram, as a very fashionable lady also waits - is the man in the street talking to the tram driver? *F. N. T. Lloyd Jones*

A Priestly bogie car approaches the crossing of West Derby Road, with the backdrop of St Margaret's Anfield. This fine church was destroyed by fire in the 1960s, and was replaced by a smaller modern design. The man on the bike is about to warily cross the junction, while two young boys stand on the traffic island. They are dressed in the short trousers of the period, which were worn by boys right up to the ages of 13 and 14!
Brian Martin collection

In 1947 - still in the old livery of red and cream - Standard car 594 trundles along Shiel Road on a short working to Rotunda, a name that had survived although the former Music Hall, at the north end of Scotland Road, had long since disappeared. The tram is demonstrating the Liverpool habit of showing the number blinds turned half-and-half to signify a short-working. Ahead of the tram is a parked Morris car with the registration DLV 500. *A. C. Noon*

LIVERPOOL TRAMS 1945-1957

Priestly bogie car 780 keeps its eye open upon the scene at the junction of Durning Road and Tunnel Road on the Outer Circular route, crossing the tracks of routes 4 and 4W in Wavertree Road. Sadly all the shops in the scene, except the Co-op building seen to the right of 780, are today long since demolished. *Martin Jenkins*

Two Marks bogie cars pass on the loop in Tunnel Road; 851 on the right sports a new livery introduced by recent Manager W. M. Hall, while the other car is still in the grimy wartime state. The terraced houses on the left went in the 1960s slum clearance programme, but the wall on the corner of Spekeland Road is still in situ today. The pub on the other corner still survived in business until recently. A lady and her small daughter alight from 851 and walk to the pavement, with no sign of other road traffic to endanger them in those days! *N. N. Forbes, NTM*

Baby Grand 222 stands at the tram stop loading passengers in Lodge Lane, at the Fern Grove and Bentley Road passing loop. The lady to the right of the tram looks as though she's just alighted, and is waiting for the approaching car to pass. On the left a man and woman are out for a stroll, enjoying the sunshine, in the attire of the period. On the right kerb a group of men meander to their favourite pub on Lodge Lane, of which there were plenty from which to choose! *J. H. Roberts*

A Priestly bogie car waits at the traffic lights at the continuation of Lodge Lane and Sefton Park Road. The tram is about to turn right into Croxteth Road to join trams on the 15 route towards Princess Park Gates and onward into the city. The devastation on this corner was bomb damage from the notorious Blitz, but by the 1960s was rebuilt. Notice that the tram stop is on the same corner as the traffic lights, a sure sign that trams in those days were unhindered by road traffic! Pedestrians cross the road with absolute safety, and a group are boarding the inbound 26. A cyclist pedals away to complete an unhurried scene. *J. H. Roberts*

With the war-ravaged Customs House on the left, a Streamliner has just rounded the curve from South Castle Street and is seen in Canning Place with South John Street in the background. Two men, one with a parcel, cross the road maybe to join the cluster of men on the pavement. Just to the right was the former Gordon Smith Seaman's Institute, a hostel for seafarers. This picture typifies the immediate post-war years in Liverpool. Today all this area has been redeveloped, with the new Steers House occupying the site of the Custom House. *Brian Martin collection*

A well-kept Standard car 26 - appropriately numbered for the Outer Circular route - with a clear side-indicator blind stands at South Castle Street terminus. On the left can be seen buildings in Harrington Street, across the bombed site at the corner of Lord Street and Castle Street. To the right a brick wall surrounds a bombed site, where now stands Refuge Assurance House. *I. R. Davidson*

LIVERPOOL TRAMS 1945-1957

15 CROXTETH ROAD

Streamliner 990 is operating on the short route 15 to Croxteth Road. Notice the juxtaposition of the destination and 'via' blinds on the side of the tram; the idea behind this experiment was that kerbside passengers could read more easily the tram's destination. Lord Street is the location, looking towards Paradise Street and Bunney's Corner, with the long-established British Home Stores to the left, which is still in the same location today but bearing the more modern 'BHS' logo. This location was an important tram stop for outbound passengers, with many routes passing along this street. A man with his raincoat over his arm and two ladies await their particular route to take them home. A very fine car is fitted between the tram and a 76 Huyton bus at the traffic lights. *A. S. Clayton*

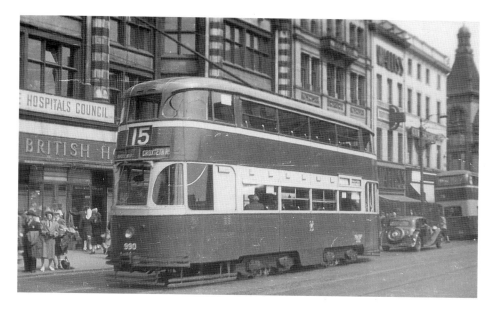

A Marks bogie car is just entering Croxteth Road on route 15, at the end of its very short journey from the city. Prince's Park is to the right, and diverging to the right the linking tracks that passed along Devonshire Road, used only for emergency and depot journeys to and from Dingle. The fine large former merchants' houses still have the same appearance today, except that many are split into apartments. Indeed, this particular scene remains intact, apart from the trams and their tracks and overhead. *N. N. Forbes, NTM*

The 15 terminus at Croxteth Road, with Cabin Car 784 on the terminal stub ready for its return to Pier Head on 14 May 1949 - the last day of operation. The new bus stops are already in position for the following day. The 15 tram route was abandoned before the war because of its short distance and a parallel bus route that went beyond this point - via Ullet Road - but reinstated with the onset of hostilities. The replacement 15 bus was soon after renumbered 80E and lost its former identity. On the left a man, woman and schoolboy await buses travelling beyond the tram terminus. The church on the corner of Brompton Avenue was recently demolished to make space for luxury flats. *A. S. Clayton*

Cross-City route 49 was an unusual service that ran completely in the outer suburbs, linking the East Lancashire Road routes with trams at the south end of the city. In this picture a Baby Grand has its trolley turned at Penny Lane ready for the return journey to Muirhead Avenue East. Note the rare facing crossover that allows trams to stand at the outward tracks ready for departure, as well as fitting in with the tracks in the foreground leading to Prince Alfred Road Depot. In the distance to the right of the tram is the shelter in the middle of the roundabout, with its well-known Beatles connotations of later years! Here buses are evident on tram replacement routes, but much of this scene remains the same today (*below left*), apart from Prince Alfred Road Depot on the right, the site of which is now occupied by the Kwik Save supermarket. *H. B. Priestley, NTM/Steve Palmer*

Just a few hundred yards up from Penny Lane terminus was the first tram stop in Church Road, where Baby Grand 271 is seen rolling down the incline. A young boy on a bicycle looks back up Norwich Road, while on the opposite corner a lady in a shawl looks round. Again this scene remains unchanged, except that the trees have flourished! *Richard Wiseman*

Above Baby Grand 223 waits for its solitary passenger to board before ascending Mill Lane to the brow of the hill at Deverell Road. Centre right is the bulk of the Abbey Cinema and the famous Picton Clock and 'lock-up'. Upon the hill to the left is Olive Mount Children's Hospital. Across the road on the left, behind the wall, today there stands Wavertree Heights and Lance Lane in the distance. Three ladies stroll down the hill, two of them wearing the popular headscarves of the period. A Bedford lorry approaches the tram and passes a parked Standard Vanguard estate, while the children's playing field behind them is still there today. *Richard Wiseman*

Right Short workings on the Penny Lane service area were run from the Edge Lane industrial area, and showed the number 42. Baby Grand 203 is seen here in Mill Lane at Deverell Road where there was a crossover and a feeder box, the cables from which can be seen to the left of the tram. The crossover was never used, even in emergencies, and even though 42 and 49 routes were abandoned in September 1952, the overhead wires were retained to this feeder right until the end of tram operation in Edge Lane in September 1957. This part of Mill Lane consisted of several roads of well-designed Liverpool Corporation houses, products of the enlightened housing policy of the 1920s. Mill Lane was also noticeable for its superb tarmac paving - from gutter to gutter - while the trams rode smoothly over the well-laid tracks. *Richard Wiseman*

Right Baby Grand 272 is seen negotiating the points at Edge Lane Drive to turn into Mill Lane on the last day of route 49, 4 September 1952. Trams on the 6A and 40 routes continued ahead on to the reserved track, the first in Liverpool, opened in 1914. In 1952 Robinson's gas meter works occupied the site on the left, which today is Peugeot dealer Edge Mill Motors. A lady waits for a 49 tram going the other way at the Mill Lane stop, and a man on his bike waits for the tram to turn the corner and keeps an eye on the Morris car emerging from the left! *Richard Wiseman*

LIVERPOOL TRAMS 1945-1957

Baby Grand 204 traverses the original curves from Edge Lane Drive into St Oswald's Street while an inspector watches the track gang working on the newly conceived Edge Lane Roundabout. The former tracks from St Oswald's Street to Edge Lane have been severed to allow the new tracks to be inserted. As it happened, the roundabout was only used by the 49 route for a matter of months, whereupon the trams were converted to buses. The brick wall in the background surrounded a Liverpool Corporation yard, where winter salt was stored as well as being a depot for the peculiar horse-drawn bin lorries. The trailers - but not the horses! - were winched on to Maudsley lorries for the journey to the land-fill site. *B. Dutton*

Standard 726 stands at the top of Edge Lane on an industrial journey, route 47 from Edge Lane to Muirhead Avenue. In front is Standard 12, bound for Page Moss, and erroneously displaying 29B on its blind! It is June 1951, with the new tram roundabout taking shape. New tracks are already in place on the left, together with the overhead wires. Meanwhile the two trams use the existing tracks, 726 to turn left into St Oswald's Street and 12 to go straight across into Edge Lane Drive. Part of the massive workforce from the Edge Lane industrial estate wend their way home on their bikes, using the temporary one-way inward lane. *N. N. Forbes, NTM*

The upper half of St Oswald's Street was improved in 1946 and took the form of a well-laid track in the latest tarmac with centre poles on an island. Just prior to the war several streets on the left were demolished to make way for the new St Oswald's Gardens tenements, only to be demolished in 1996! On the right the old streets of Hurst Street and part of Macqueen Street disappeared to make way for the new Hurst Gardens. Rotherham's pawnbrokers is the first shop on the right, followed by a green-grocer, a butcher, two general stores and another butcher beyond. St Oswald's Roman Catholic Church spire and the old school buildings can be seen in the middle distance. In the centre of the scene a 47 tram heads outwards to Muirhead Avenue East. *Richard Wiseman*

LIVERPOOL TRAMS 1945-1957

Peak-hour service cars on the 49 for Penny Lane and the 47 for Edge Lane pass Green Lane Depot in 1952, bearing the sign for pedestrians to 'Beware of the Cars'. A devastating fire had occurred five years earlier in 1947 and had resulted in only one of the two depot entrances still being used by the trams; the one seen here was used by buses on the 10 and 10C. An Austin 12 follows behind 226, while the hoardings on the corner of Green Lane and Prescot Road advertise the Gaumont Cinema, Bar One and Player's cigarettes, dominated above by Beecham's Pills! The building on the left is now demolished along with the tram depot, succumbing to the demolition men in 1995. *Richard Wiseman*

On their way to the eastern suburbs, the 49 trams traversed the length of Green Lane from Prescot Road to West Derby Road, sharing the tracks with route 11. Here 873 is photographed when Prince Alfred Road Depot worked the route; after its closure on 11 December 1949 the route was worked by Edge Lane. Brand new tracks are being laid, and the stacks of sets are ready to be replaced in readiness for the tarred bonding infill. A mother and daughter pass, oblivious to the track improvements, at the corner of Rockbank Road. *H. B. Priestley, NTM*

Usually only reaching Muirhead Avenue East on their normal duties, the 49s were extended during peak periods to Kirkby Trading Estate and No 5 gate. Here a 49 tram is seen heading back towards the south end along Boundary Road. Today all traces of the tramway have disappeared and the area abounds with factories; in tram days the factories were confined to the limits of the trading estate at Kirkby. *D. A. Thompson*

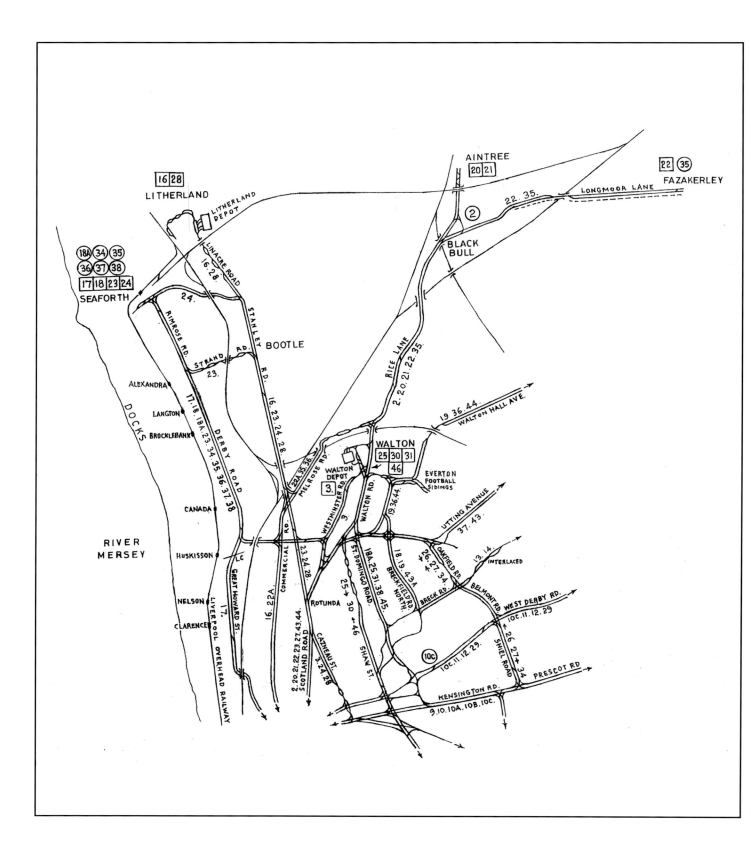

16 LITHERLAND 28

Litherland tram terminus was the end of the line for trams on the 16 route to Pier Head and the 28 route to Lime Street; it was a dead-end adjacent to Litherland station on the Southport electric line. The two routes shared tracks as far as Bank Hall, then the 16s reached the City via Commercial Road and Vauxhall Road while the 28s went via Stanley Road, Scotland Road and Cazneau Street to Lime Street. *N. N. Forbes, NTM*

Heading for the Old Haymarket, Standard EMB 305 heads away from Litherland terminus along Bridge Road at Wellington Road, having just left the Beach Road passing loop. It is now approaching the passing loop on the curve into Linacre Road. All the property on the left was subsequently demolished to make way for the A5036 extension, Princess Way. *N. N. Forbes, NTM*

Marks bogie car 848, on route 16 via Vauxhall Road, is seen passing one of several hostelries, a Walkers pub, on the corner of Hopwood Street, which was popular with its close proximity to the dockside industry. Lightbody Street to the left led to Clarence Dock and Nelson Dock Overhead Railway stations, and the Liverpool locks of the Leeds & Liverpool Canal. *N. N. Forbes, NTM*

A nostalgic scene on Vauxhall Road, as a Priestly Standard car on the 16 route heading for Pier Head passes under Liverpool's own 'Bridge of Sighs'. These startling footbridges with their ornate architecture linked the streetside factories of Tate & Lyle, the Liverpool company of sugar and syrup fame. Unfortunately these features have since been demolished and the site redeveloped, although the Tate Gallery in London and Albert Dock in Liverpool can be visited today for artistic works! *N. N. Forbes, NTM*

18   SEAFORTH   17

Standard 305 reposes at Seaforth terminus behind a Baby Grand on the 18 route. While the Baby Grand is still in the pre-war livery and looks down at heel, 305 has obviously received a fairly recent repaint! The posters are interesting - a Royal Navy recruiting poster sharing the wall-space with a Communist Party rally, where William Gallagher MP is going to speak at Liverpool Stadium. *Martin Jenkins collection*

A Marks bogie car emerges from beneath the Liverpool-Southport railway line in Chadwick Street on tracks that connected Pall Mall with Great Howard Street. This area was well-supplied with warehouses serving the nearby docks. Two young boys watch the tram as it passes by - perhaps they are budding tram enthusiasts? St Augustine's RC Church in Great Howard Street, beyond the bridge, was demolished in 1976. *N. N. Forbes, NTM*

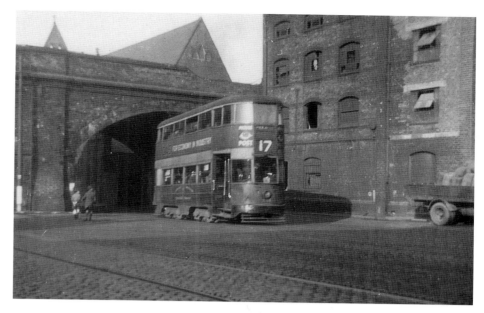

Always a hive of activity was the Commercial Road/Sandhills Lane/Lambeth Road junction. Standard 81 is bound for Breckfield Road on route 18, while a Standard on route 16 passes in the background. One of the open-staircase buses is seeing service in post-war years bound for Old Swan, on what later became route 67. A lady holding her hat rushes across the road, while a group of workers wait for the next bus. Note a railway goods line crossing the tram tracks in the foreground on Sandhills Lane! *N. N. Forbes, NTM*

A peak-hour 18A on a dockers' special for Seaforth crosses the junction of Lambeth Road and Commercial Road. Standard 577 is still in the old pre-war colours of red and cream, and is sporting the pre-fab windscreen that was fitted to many open-platform cars in the late 1940s. Two cyclists wait for the tram to pass, while the corner shop of E. R. Allen is adorned with several tobacco advertisements. The legend in the bottom of the shop window proclaims 'Lighter Repair Service'. *N. N. Forbes, NTM*

Baby Grand 285 - still with original 1939-style indicator numerals - awaits departure for Lime Street at Seaforth terminus. Off-duty dock workers on the left seem to be waiting for another tram, while a Ribble bus from the Crosby direction turns into Knowsley Road from Crosby Road South. The conical-roofed hostelry on the right is one of Threlfall's houses, a local brewery, and is advertising 'Blue Label'. *A. D. Packer*

In 1949 routes 23, 24 and 28 cars were transferred to South Castle Street terminus, enabling Cazneau Street, St Anne Street and Norton Street to be abandoned. There they took the place of trams on routes 10 to Prescot and 12 to West Derby, converted to buses in June and May respectively. Here Standard 746 on route 40 shows Clayton Square on its blind, obviously not having a 'Castle Street' to show. Post-war rebuilding is under way, with the site for Refuge Assurance House and the steel framework for the buildings in Lord Street. *N. N. Forbes, NTM*

The Queen Victoria monument in South Castle Street forms the backdrop to Standard 729 on route 24 to Seaforth, with a solitary passenger on the top deck! This picture shows the length of the trolley and its rope to facilitate turning by its conductor. Note also the swivel trolley-head, which is able to work at an angle, and the wiring loop to secure it from falling and causing injury! *Brian Martin collection*

LIVERPOOL TRAMS 1945-1957

Marks bogie car 856 heads down the slope at the Black Bull, bound for the city from Aintree in November 1951. This was a period just after the abandonment of route 21 to Aintree and 22 to Fazakerley in August of that year, when route 2 as a peak-hour special to Black Bull was extended to Aintree until November. Keeping trams on route 2 to Aintree enabled the LCPT to secure an extra bus licence on the Walton-Aintree corridor, in competition with Ribble! In this scene - a finale - notice that the trolley wires to the right are still in place on the abandoned route 22. To the left is Warbreck station on the Cheshire Lines railway, adorned with travel notices, and a group of passengers await services beyond the city. The road to Aintree is busy and a bus stands at the Black Bull terminus outside the pub of that name. *N. N. Forbes, NTM*

Baby Grand 216, bound for Black Bull on route 2, heads outwards along the pre-war track of Rice Lane in July 1951. A Rover is parked on the left, while two boys on bikes take a breather! Liverpool's modern type of centre-bracket poles on islands add to the neat road scene. *H. B. Priestley, NTM*

A delightful scene near St Mary's Parish Church on County Road, Walton, with Cabin Car 816 heading inwards for Pier Head in November 1951. Most of the motor cars are pre-war models, including a Rover and a Wolseley, while to the left of the tram is a brand-new Singer SM1500. A lady in a headscarf waits to cross the road with a parcel under her arm, while two men on bikes pause for a chat. *N. N. Forbes, NTM*

A wartime scene at Aintree terminus, with Marks bogie car 856 waiting for 795 to reverse from the stub - note the white-painted buffers and headlamp masks. 795 began life as a Cabin Car, but was destroyed by fire in 1935 and rebuilt as a Marks car. The Liverpool custom of leaving number indicators showing half of each number to signify a short or depot journey is being demonstrated by 795. An assortment of pedestrians in the road seem to indicate the sparseness of motor traffic in those days! *N. N. Forbes, NTM*

Aintree terminus on a quite afternoon in 1948, showing the end of the line that marked the Liverpool City boundary. The Sefton Arms on the corner and, just beyond it, the entrance to Aintree race-course provide the backdrop for English Electric bogie car 766 awaiting its return to Aigburth. The traditional cobbles of the road surface are replaced by smooth tarmac across the border in Lancashire. This distinguished Liverpool streets in post-war years until the tram tracks were removed, or relaid on some routes. *R. B. Parr, NTM*

Priestly bogie car 775, coming from the Aintree terminus, is seen at Wyresdale Road, with the railway bridge in the background, during the autumn of 1951 when route 2 was extended. A policeman with a cape over the handlebars of his bicycle is perhaps going on duty, and waits for the tram and another cyclist to pass. The corner chemist proudly announces 'National Health Service Dispensing' on its window, while another shop has its sun blind extended to shade its window display. *Brian Martin collection*

RACES

Aintree is a world-famous racecourse, and on race days the simple terminal stub would become a tram bottleneck! Here Marks bogie car 853 on service 20 - Aintree and Aigburth Vale - gets tangled up with race 'specials'. Displaying the legend 'RACES' on its indicator, a red and cream 709 waits while a policeman allows passengers to alight from the front platform of the service car. In this 1947 scene, another Standard car can be seen as a 'special', reversing on the terminal stub. *F. N. T. Lloyd Jones*

Standard 84 heads a line of nine trams awaiting homeward-bound race-goers at the Aintree terminus. Bound for Aigburth Vale on route 21, it looks like the lull before the storm! Indeed, this group of trams is ready to transport the 1950 Grand National punters homewards. *E. A. Gahan*

The races are over, and race-goers start the trek home, while a normal tram on route 21 - Streamliner 932 - waits to reverse in a queue of 'specials'. A policeman is ready to regulate the traffic, as a man and boy cross to the kerb with their fish and chips! *R. F. Mack, John Fozard collection*

The old offices of the Liverpool *Daily Post and Echo* in Whitechapel are passed by Priestly Standard car 84 bound for Aigburth Vale. It is July 1950, a fine day bringing out printers to sit in the sun for their break. A motor cyclist - without crash helmet - prepares to pass the tram, while a new Austin Devon van follows behind. Visible on the right is the City College of Technology, near to the Old Haymarket and Mersey Tunnel entrance. *N. N. Forbes, NTM*

Streamliner 958 enters Whitechapel at what was popularly known as 'Bunney's Corner', Liverpool's 'Holy crossing' - the junction of Lord Street, Church Street, Whitechapel and Paradise Street, on route 21 from Aintree to Aigburth. Here Opposite Bunney's department store was the gentleman's outfitters Hope Brothers. Today Macdonald's and Mothercare adorn the junction. *A. H. Jacob*

Signifying a short journey to Dingle, Standard 679 shows half 20 and half 21 on its blind, and is seen heading outwards from the city along St James Street - the back way! To the left is Jamaica Street, with a distant view of the Liver Building and the spire of the Swedish Church, while on the right a man brushes the gutters as boys pass. *N. N. Forbes, NTM*

LIVERPOOL TRAMS 1945-1957

DINGLE 21

The Ancient Chapel of Toxteth is prominent as a tram on route 20 to Aigburth Vale rounds the corner from Park Road to Ullet Road. Behind the photographer is the Dingle station of the Liverpool Overhead Railway, while just to the right of the tram is the junction for city-bound trams via Beloe Street and Mill Street, routes 21 and 45. *J. H. Roberts*

Dingle Mount, on Dingle Lane curve, with 716 running into Dingle sheds in the background, showing 20A/21 on its blind. Baby Grand 203 on route 21 is heading for Aintree via the city; is it loading passengers here? The spire of Toxteth Congregational Church can be seen in the distance to the left of 716. *N. N. Forbes, NTM*

AIGBURTH VALE 20

Aigburth Vale terminus, compared with the cramped conditions at Aintree, was palatial! A three-track layout permitted the laying over of cars without hindering through trams to Garston. Here Cabin Car 783 and Standard 693 prepare for their return journey to Aintree. The adjacent lines of shops were always busy, as indeed they still are today! An Inspector keeps a watchful eye on the proceedings, as 693 disgorges its passengers. *Brian Martin collection*

Marks car 848 is seen on route 22 bound for Fazakerley, at the junction of Tithebarn Street, Vauxhall Road and Great Crosshall Street. Here points have been laid for a proposed line straight ahead in Marybone and Bevington Hill, which would have shortened the journey that 848 is about to make via Great Crosshall Street, Byrom Street and Scotland Road. Prouts Garage is behind the tram, while the LCPT head office is just to the right in Hatton Garden. *N. N. Forbes, NTM*

Returning to Pier Head from Fazakerley is Priestly bogie car 771, on the side reservation in Longmoor Lane at First Avenue. A cluster of little shops cater for all needs - the first on the right offers Ovaltine, a favourite of this post-war period. The Chase Hotel is on the left, where the road narrows and the tram tracks cross the narrow bridge over the railway at Fazakerley station. *J. H. Roberts*

Looking citywards at Fazakerley from another tram as Priestly bogie car 775 arrives at the terminus. Passengers are already alighting, while down the road can be seen a new AEC bus on route 87, which in 1949 ran every 40 minutes from Fazakerley to Kings Drive - Stockbridge Lane - via Kirkby Trading Estate. This scene typifies Liverpool town planning with a tram reservation, carriageways and pavements, complete with grass verges and trees, all giving an air of spaciousness and organisation. Longmoor Lane is lined by Corporation housing; the library can be seen on the left and cottage homes were sited on the right. *H. B. Priestley, NTM*

Another view showing the end of the line, the overhead strung off and two trams - including Marks bogie car 843 - next to the shelter. If trams had been able to continue ahead they could have connected with trams on the 19 route to Kirkby! This is the city boundary, and old farm buildings can be seen amongst the trees; these were later replaced by Fazakerley playing fields. *K. G. Harvie*

30   WALTON   31

In 1948 Baby Grand 227, still in pre-war livery, ascends St Domingo Road on route 31 from Walton to the Pier Head. Centre poles decorate the centre of the road on this section, while the hoardings that surround Electricity Department property provide colour: 'Splendid! Cadbury's Blended', 'My Goodness - My Guinness' and 'How can I ease my troublesome cough?' At the bottom of the hill can be seen Notre Dame Convent at the Everton Valley and Kirkdale Vale intersection. *N. N. Forbes, NTM*

Pictured at the bottom of Lord Street, amidst the post-war bombed areas of the city, are two cars on route 31. Outward-bound is Standard 342 passing a Cabin Car in pre-war livery, while bringing up the rear is a Streamliner on route 19. The comprehensive tracks in the foreground allowed access into Castle Street to the left and South Castle Street to the right, with the terminus around the Queen Victoria monument. Miraculously surviving the Blitz was Lancaster House in the centre; the premises of Posts & Telegraphs, it was eventually demolished in 1990. *MTPS*

=THE NORTH EASTERN ROUTES=

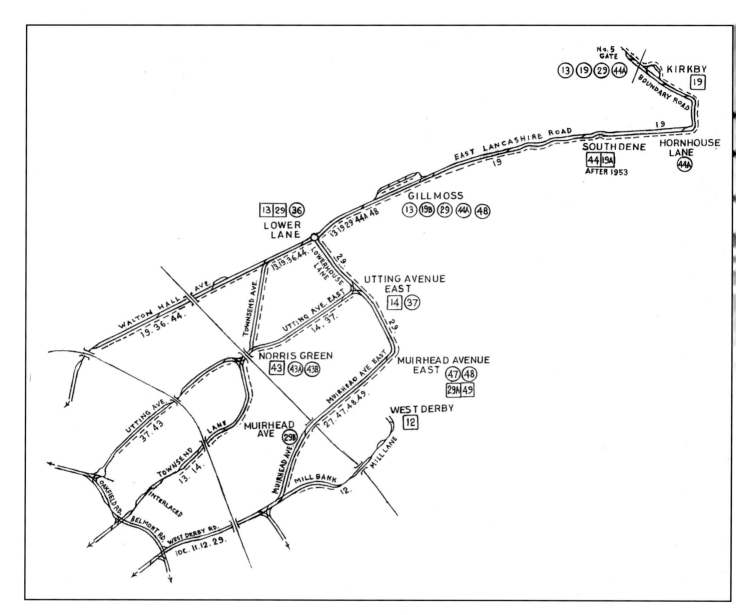

Pier Head in 1951, with the Cunard Building decorated for the Festival of Britain. An Inspector paces towards the trams, Standard 98 on route 29A and Marks car 824 on route 31 to Walton. *F. Mussett*

Routes 19 and 44

A busy scene in Elliot Street in April 1952, showing pavements crowded with shoppers, Streamliner 155 and an Albion Guinness lorry waiting at the pedestrian crossing. On the left-hand side is the old St John's Market, while opposite is Blackler's store and Timpson's shoe shop. Today this is a pedestrian precinct landscaped in tiers, with the entrance to the modern St John's Precinct; on the right is also a completely new 1987 building housing Boots. The ABC Cinema at the corner of Lime Street is still there today as the Cannon. Today people can stroll through this area, now free from traffic - note the young trees, neat litter bins and pigeons. Undoubtedly this is an age when crowds of shoppers in city centres want to be separated from busy traffic - and the trams of the 1950s! *H. B. Priestley/Steve Palmer*

A lovely view from the front seat on a service tram in Walton Hall Avenue, with service 19 tram 253 approaching from Kirkby, and the long straight reservation stretching out in front. Seen in the spring, the trees are bare and there is little traffic on the road; the railway bridge carries the former Cheshire Lines railway. *Brian Martin*

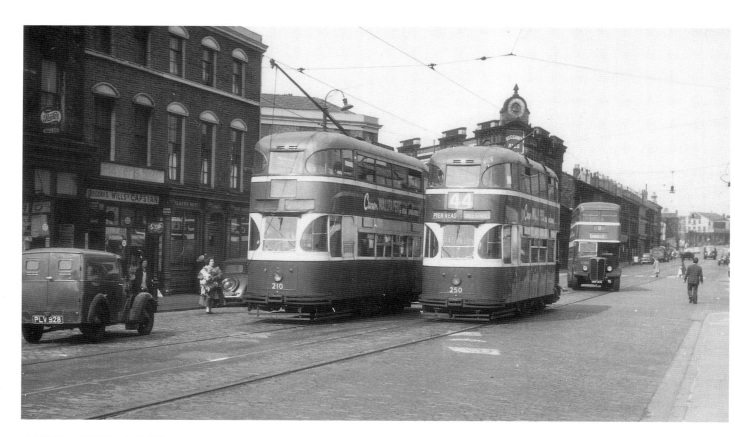

LIVERPOOL TRAMS 1945-1957

Left In Kirkdale Road - Everton Valley - two Baby Grands pass each other: 210 is returning to Walton Depot and 250 is bound for Pier Head on route 44. They are followed by an AEC bus on route 3 bound for Dingle, having replaced trams since 1948. Behind tram 250 is a Higson's Ales public house, while at the tram stop is a Pepsi-Cola snack bar and Gregson's newspaper shop. Looking at Kirkdale Road's surface, the cobbles have been skimmed with tar for smoother riding. *Richard Wiseman*

Below left A busy scene before the Northern Post Office - at the foot of Everton Valley - as a rush hour begins with the arrival of a Baby Grand tram on 44A and the Daimler bus on 22A, bound for 'GT CROSSHALL ST'. They have just travelled three-quarters of a mile from Walton Depot along Walton Road. The Walker's Ales Derby Arms public house on the corner with Kirkdale Road boasted a very elegant doorway, but today is demolished. The white-coated policeman is on traffic-duty, but the cyclists turning right cannot see him at the moment, hidden by the tram. The van behind seems to have an old fireplace in the back! *Pam Eaton*

Top right A picturesque view from a service 44 tram in Scotland Road, showing the width of the road accommodating the loading islands for the tram stops. There is a large crowd waiting for the approaching tram bound for Southdene, including the children who will be entitled to a 1d return ticket. Unfortunately this did not apply on the buses, represented here by one on the 27 route from Seaforth. The cars - modern Austin and Morris Minor - are stopped for the pedestrian crossing outside the Throstle's Nest. Scotland Road was famous for having a public house on every corner! St Anthony's RC Church stands back behind its railings and notice board between the pub and funeral director Daly & Co Ltd. *R. B. Parr, NTM*

Middle right A striking view of Islington Square in April 1954, at the junction of Shaw Street and West Derby Road, with two Streamliners, 883 and 186, on routes 19 and 14 respectively. This is a busy location with varied transport, including the bare-headed motor cyclist, the cyclist making a hand-signal and the parked Armstrong Siddeley car outside the Walker's pub. Skulnick's wallpaper shop is next door to Gascoign's newsagents, surmounted by a poster advising us to 'Have a Guinness when you're tired'. *H. B Priestley, NTM*

Right Here is a one-way system on route 19 - while 178 goes along Eastbourne Street, 186 returns along Fitzclarence Street. The three-storey houses, seen here in 1954, are now demolished and replaced by Everton Park, and thus the location is indistinguishable today. Streamliner 178 is bound for Southdene, hence its 19A number for the short working. *Richard Wiseman*

Having made its way through the one-way system in Everton Valley, Streamliner 880 travels along Breckfield Road North towards Walton on 13 April 1954. It is passing St Domingo Methodist Church, while opposite is Everton Scriptural Church. It is interesting to note that the feeder cable is suspended centrally by the span wires, which are also supporting the street lights. Clearly this is a smoothly surfaced road for 18 inches on each side of the tram track, following re-laying. *H. B. Priestley, NTM*

A very nostalgic view of Streamliner 869 (since preserved) in April 1954, turning from Anfield Road into Walton Lane in front of the imposing Stanley Park Evangelical Church. The traditional school road-sign on the left warns that Walton Technical College is in this area, on the 19 route. The cobbles in the foreground have been replaced by tarmac round the curve into Sleepers Hill, thus indicating that the track has been re-laid. *H. B. Priestley, NTM*

Here is a view in Walton Lane, where the tram track is situated in a side reservation next to the grounds of Stanley Park. While Streamliner 187, en route from Kirkby, waits at the stop, workmen attending to a rail joint stand back to allow it to pass. This is the junction with Spellow Lane, with emergency track leading to nearby Walton Depot. In the foreground is a crossover that can be used by trams in emergencies. A Bedford lorry approaches, passing an interesting cycle shop on the corner advertising Raleigh bicycles. *H. B. Priestley, NTM*

Looking down Walton Lane, 174 is on route 44 for Southdene, passing a row of trams on the Everton Football Club sidings, but stored here after the fire at Walton Depot in March 1954. Headed by Baby Grand 210, ten trams are alongside the rather picturesque fence and trees of Stanley Park. The track in the foreground - set traditionally in cobbles - leads from the disused depot-only track in Spellow Lane. *H. B. Priestley, NTM*

A view from the spur in Priory Road, used for reversing football specials, as a tram on route 19 passes on Walton Lane in April 1954, with Everton football ground in the background. In the foreground is Stubbs, monumental sculptor, with samples on display behind the fence. The central traction pole on the island on the right is distinctive with its black and white stripes, and carries the signposts left to CITY, MERSEY TUNNEL and right to MANCHESTER. *H. B. Priestley, NTM*

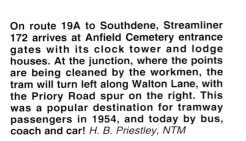

On route 19A to Southdene, Streamliner 172 arrives at Anfield Cemetery entrance gates with its clock tower and lodge houses. At the junction, where the points are being cleaned by the workmen, the tram will turn left along Walton Lane, with the Priory Road spur on the right. This was a popular destination for tramway passengers in 1954, and today by bus, coach and car! *H. B. Priestley, NTM*

Trams 162 and 903 are seen on routes 19A and 44 in Walton village heading for the East Lancashire Road. At the corner of Cherry Lane can be seen a pawnbroker, while the man on his bike waits until the tram passes, perhaps unaware that a Leyland Comet lorry is approaching him! A rather elegant Jaguar of that era - April 1954 - is turning right. If you miss the tram, cars are for hire on the right over by the two parked Standard Vanguards. *H. B. Priestley, NTM*

On East Lancashire Road, with its lovely central reservation for the trams, Streamliner 973 heads for the city, watched by a lady and her daughter, in April 1955. The junction with Townsend Avenue, for trams on route 13 bound for Lower Lane, is immediately behind the photographer. *R. B. Parr, NTM*

At Gillmoss, where there was a trading estate including the large English Electric factory, there was a long two-track siding with queue barriers where trams could wait for the workers. Here is Baby Grand 258 on route 13A for Old Haymarket, several other trams and a bus waiting at their respective barriers. A service tram - bound for Kirkby - can be seen passing on the central reservation in the background. Today the thin layers of tarmac covering the rails are wearing away to reveal one of the few surviving relics of the tramway era in Liverpool! *Richard Wiseman*

A busy scene on the main line at Gillmoss, where there is a long queue for the city as 231 arrives from the siding on route 14 via Islington. Baby Grand 270 is leaving the stop for Kirkby, while a lot of loaded lorries pass on the road. The Council estate, built in the 1950s, can be seen over the heads of the queue - are the group in the centre looking for someone? *Richard Wiseman*

A rural scene as 248 passes the farm at Radshaw Nook. In 1956 there was a crossing for the farm, but 40 years later the M57 motorway crosses the East Lancashire Road at this point - although there is still space for trams! Looking down as you pass, the remaining tram track can be seen still set in a special bridge over Knowsley Brook. *N. N. Forbes/Steve Palmer*

Outside the city boundary, Southdene terminus, for trams on routes 19A and 44, was created in 1953, the former being extended from Gillmoss on 17 May and the latter on 7 December. This was to serve the new housing estate, built on the left-hand side, and in the background can be seen a diversion in the tramway for a proposed roundabout, which was never built. The residents of the new estate built their own 'wind break' as a shelter from the elements, and after negotiating for two years with the Passenger Transport Department, a concrete shelter was built. *Roy Brook*

A striking scene at Hornhouse Lane crossover, with Marks bogie car 841 returning to Lower Lane, and probably Walton Depot. The East Lancashire Road service was extended to the city boundary in 1942, to Hornhouse Lane in October 1943, and finally to ROF Kirkby in December of that year. While the busy East Lancashire Road continues ahead, the tram will turn left towards Kirkby Trading Estate and the terminus there. A traffic island has been built here, at the junction with Ormskirk Road, and there is a light tram shelter with one passenger. In the distance can be seen an RAC booth by the layby, while there are warning lights for the oncoming trams in the foreground. *H. B. Priestley, NTM*

The passengers are leaving 187, having just arrived from Pier Head at the tram stop on Boundary Road in Kirkby; the housing estate of the 1950s is on the left, there is a factory chimney on the right and the potatoes are growing well in the field. Note that the crossover has been used by a tram whose wheels have become derailed. This 1950s scene proves that trams provided a splendid service for the residents of Kirkby, using exclusive reservation for speed and efficiency! *R. F. Mack, A. D. Packer collection*

Leaving Kirkby - and the housing estate - is 253, as it turns the corner from Boundary Road at Hornhouse Lane, bound for Pier Head. The 19 route trams provided a useful service to the city for the residents of this leafy outpost surrounded by fields. *Pam Eaton*

Two children standing at the tram stop admire Streamliner 984 returning to the city on route 19. Note the flexible suspension of the overhead on the centre bracket poles, which was designed for the conversion of the trolley poles to bow-collectors on the trams, which move was prevented by the war. The pole in the foreground carries a signal light system, to warn trams of traffic crossing from the farm. *H. B. Priestley, NTM*

Routes 13 and 14

Looking under Clubmoor Bridge of the Cheshire Lines railway at Norris Green on 10 April 1954, car 154 is turning right on the 14 route into Utting Avenue East. It is a spectacular view along the reservation, with the bracket poles carrying the street lights on the dual carriageway and suspending the tramway overhead between them. A modern public library faces the junction, while the shop opposite shares the 1930s style of the buildings. Ladies push their prams across the tram lines past lamps of contrasting styles, gas and electric. *H. B. Priestley, NTM*

UTTING AVE EAST

Utting Avenue East - terminal of route 14 - is seen here with Marks bogie car 841 having its trolley turned by the conductor. Priestly bogie car is on a peak-hour working on route 13A, which is turning for Old Haymarket. The tramway junction here comprised a left turn into Lower House Lane and right into Dwerryhouse Lane, securing flexibility for peak-hour operation. *Martin Jenkins collection*

Today the remains of this tramway terminus can still be distinguished, with three of the original poles. The tall blocks of flats, housing and the Western Approaches public house were developed in the 1960s. *Steve Palmer*

The 'Walker's Ales' sign dominates the railway bridge of the LNWR Bootle branch line in Townsend Lane, under which 973's trolley swings sideways to clear the roof of the tram, and an Albion lorry passes. To brighten this rather gloomy location, the posters supply amusement: 'Hovis is the Slice of Life', 'Lifebuoy for Health' and 'French Nights' at the Pavilion on Monday 8 August (1955). *Martin Jenkins collection*

This is the view from the bridge looking down Townsend Lane, and showing 164 leaving the exclusive reservation to get under the bridge. This line was originally extended in 1924, to serve the housing development in Norris Green. The full width of the dual carriageway was 120 feet, including 36 feet for the tramway reservation, but the widening of the railway bridges would have been too costly. Looking down here one can see the original cobbled lane, but the cyclist is riding on the nearside tarmac. *H. B. Priestley, NTM*

Streamliner 977 is on a route 13A 'special' in Everton Valley at the junction with Kirkdale Vale, coming from Walton Depot during the peak period, followed by 951 on route 44A. This photograph was taken in April 1954, when the Everton Valley track was being used by the 44 route (and by the 26 and 27 Outer Circular until 1948). In those days people's clothing - and the property - looked smarter! Certainly the three-storey houses have an attractive pattern of mottled bricks, and a basement raising the front door level. *H. B. Priestley, NTM*

Trams on routes 13 and 29 meet at Islington Square in April 1954; 170 on route 13 turns from Shaw Street, while 249 has travelled down Brunswick Road - which is one-way - on route 29. Streamliner 170, its driver standing, does seem to be leaning over on the curve, and is followed by a learner in a three-wheeler. There are eye-catching posters for Guinness, *John Bull*, *Illustrated* and *Everybody's* magazines and Player's cigarettes. *Richard Wiseman*

A busy scene in Breck Road, with the tram on route 13 loading at the pavement on a passing loop immediately in front of the shops. In the 1950s local shops offered a specialist choice of goods: look at the prices all over the greengrocer's window, the butcher, the newsagent, and the TV shop for Bush, Murphy and Ekco. The smooth road finish round the tram-lines indicates re-laying here in post-war years. Today Breck Road had been widened, and half of the shops have thus been demolished - today people use supermarkets! *R. W. A. Jones*

LIVERPOOL TRAMS 1945-1957

This is the former Tuebrook station on the Bootle branch line, and Baby Grand 218 has stopped for passengers in West Derby Road, while the traffic waits behind. Note that the trolley is nearer to this side owing to the low bridge, which carries the advice that

Cephos is 'The Physicians' Remedy', 'Safe and Certain'. West Derby Road was subsequently widened to become a dual carriageway in the 1960s. *Richard Wiseman*

Tuebrook, at the junction of West Derby Road and Green Lane, was also the junction for Muirhead Avenue to the left for the 29 route and Mill Bank for the 12 route to West Derby in the background. Streamliner 911 is bound for the city, and another tram can be seen on the cross-city route 49. By this time - June 1952 - the track to West Derby had been removed, but routes 29, 49 and 11 could be seen here. Note the traditional wider numbers on 911, the quiet Co-operative shop on the left and the 1930s flats on the far corner. *Richard Wiseman*

Car 986 on the 29A has terminated at the east end of Muirhead Avenue in the spring of 1954; route 29 trams continued via Lower House Lane to Lower Lane roundabout. Passengers are waiting in the shelter for a tram to the city, at a location just past Queens Drive which is bridged by this road. Note how the trees have had to be pruned to be clear of the overhead line. *Richard Wiseman*

Looking back towards the junction with Mill Bank, 169 has just crossed Queens Drive and is heading for Pier Head on route 29. Muirhead Avenue in the spring of 1954 does look very nostalgic - although the route closed on 3 April that year, the grass verge remains to this day. *Richard Wiseman*

Baby Grand 218 is turning into Dwerryhouse Lane on the last day of service for the route 29, with tram enthusiasts capturing the scene for ever. The cyclist, however, is heading for Oak Lane, down which is the entrance to the grounds of Croxteth Hall, now owned by Liverpool City. Playing fields can be seen through the fence, but today the land is covered by a new housing estate. *Richard Wiseman*

LIVERPOOL TRAMS 1945-1957

12 WEST DERBY

An early post-war scene on route 12 to West Derby with Standard 43 leaving the reservation on Mill Bank at Delamain Road. The driver is appropriately dressed in his hat and his raincoat, and there are no passengers enjoying the balcony on a what may be a cold summer day. It is interesting to record that a famous local resident - Roy Thomson - started a leaflet campaign to 'Save Our Trams', but route 12 was converted to buses in May 1949.
Martin Jenkins collection

A very historic scene with route 12 trams on Mill Lane, West Derby, in 1949, with St Mary's Parish Church and the entrance to the grounds of Croxteth Hall complete with rampant lions! Sadly the two trams - 299 and 170 - are still in their pre-war livery with layers of dirt and pre-war advertisements, although their indicators look cleaner. The lifeguards on Baby Grand 299 look rather battered, but the people look lively - cyclists in Almonds Green, boys playing games - and no traffic. Very nostalgic! *F. N. T. Lloyd Jones*

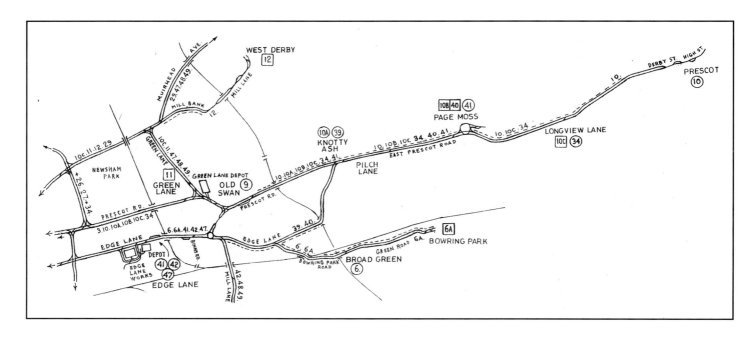

Left 'Persil for coloureds too!' is the familiar slogan in the background of this striking view from an eastbound tram, showing an evening rush hour in Edge Lane. You will notice how Baby Grands 255 and 240 show their destinations on their screens as via Edge Lane, indicating that they are 'specials'. Shining in the sun in the distance are several other Baby Grands of the Green Goddess family, which belong to the depot seen on the right. *Pam Eaton*

Below At the same location at Easter 1996, the former tram depot is now used by the buses of Merseyside Transport Ltd, and Edge Lane is now a broader dual carriageway. Some of the factories have now been replaced by a shopping centre on the right, but the Hope & Anchor public house is still there. *Steve Palmer*

Above right Streamliner 901 is seen in North John Street - terminus of route 11 - on 4 July 1953, the last day of the service. Trams came into North John Street via Dale Street, and returned via Church Street and Lime Street, proceeding along West Derby Road to Green Lane. *A. S. Clayton*

Right Standard car 451 passes Owen Owen in Clayton Square on service 11 in April 1950, in rather grubby condition. The side indicator is in the centre of the three-window saloon. These cars were rebuilt from 1935 with new seating and indicators, and then appeared in the new green and cream livery, hence the 'Green Goddess' nickname. *Richard Wiseman*

Left Streamliner 901 stands at the tram stop island in Lime Street, with Burton's and the Legs of Man public house at the corner of London Road, into which it is about to turn. A Ribble lowbridge Leyland PD2 is passing the tram, heading for the bus station in Skelhorne Street alongside Lime Street station. *A. S. Clayton*

Middle left At Grant Gardens, at the junction of Everton Road and West Derby Road, were trams on route 11 for Green Lane, 12 for West Derby and 29 for Muirhead Avenue East. Streamliner 168 - advertising Mother's Pride bread - has just left the island stop, where there is a new concrete shelter, on 8 June 1953. Outside Grant Gardens is a lorry delivering soft drinks, and the Midland Bank imposingly dominates the curve. *Richard Wiseman*

Bottom left In June 1952 Streamliner 914, on route 11, is leaving the island tram stop, complete with its 'PRESTON' signpost pointing towards Walton and Aintree. The York Hotel is on the corner of Aber Street, with the Hippodrome Cinema opposite, complete with a coat of arms surmounting the facade. It is interesting to recall that on this site was once Hengler's Circus, until it was replaced by the cinema in the 1920s. *K. A. J. Everett*

Above right At the Green Lane terminus of route 11, outside the Parish Church, 764 is showing 'NORTH JOHN ST' on its indicator, and is one of the English Electric Standards that were put into service in 1931, and later modernised. The Streamliner on route 49 - bound for Penny Lane - waits for it to move out of its way in September 1952. *Richard Wiseman*

Right 'Enjoy a Double Diamond today' says the poster at Low Hill, where Streamliner 916 on route 10B for Page Moss has reversed on a short working, and is about to turn into Kensington when the driver takes his position. The tram's traditional advert for the *Daily Telegraph* contrasts with the bright appearance of The Wallpaper Shop - being painted today - and the parked estate car. In April 1954 the Belisha beacon and pedestrian crossing are bright and clear, while the traditional property in Low Hill looks somewhat dingy - although the chimney stacks have been refurbished! *H. B. Priestley, NTM*

Left Streamliner 889 heads for the Pier Head on route 10B along Prescot Road in June 1954, and passes the former Stanley station on the Bootle branch of the LNWR. The station building was then used by H. Wilkinson & Sons, who advertised removals and storage, coal and coke, and haulage. Fairfield Police Sports Ground is on the left-hand side behind the fence, and the street lighting is suspended by span wires between the poles, making the street very neat. *Richard Wiseman*

Below left Here is a busy scene at Old Swan, as passengers board the 10B bound for Clayton Square, ushered on by the conductor holding his TIM (ticket issuing machine) box. In the foreground is the Black Horse Lane passing loop, a terminus for short workings on route 9. At the end of the Prescot Road tram reservation is the shopping centre, including the Curzon Cinema in an impressive Art Deco style. *Richard Wiseman*

10B PAGE MOSS

Top right Streamliner 950 is racing a lorry over the Cheshire Lines railway bridge at Knotty Ash station on East Prescot Road in June 1954. The Ovaltine lady is asleep on the poster next to the station entrance and above the wall-mounted letterbox. The 10B service tram is heading for Page Moss on a 20-minute headway, following the closure of the 10C to Longview Lane in June 1952. At this time the 10B and 41 trams were based at Edge Lane Depot, following the closure of Green Lane Depot to trams in April 1954. Today the railway line is a cycle path and the tramway is a grassed reservation in the centre of the dual carriageway - happy memories! *Richard Wiseman*

Middle right This photograph depicts perfectly the central reservation on East Prescot Road, with a straight run to Page Moss for Streamliner 897 in April 1954. Having just cleared the Pilch Lane crossover - used by trams on route 40 turning for Edge Lane Depot at night - this tram will now increase speed and beat the bus, followed by a lorry and a Morris Minor. They are passing Dovecot prefabs, which provided accommodation following the war. *H. B. Priestley, NTM*

Right Cars 168 and 238 stand at Page Moss terminus, which is in the form of a turning circle for the trams on routes 10B and 40, although the crossover could be used by a tram driver if necessary. Separate shelters for stops are provided for passengers travelling on 40 along Edge Lane or 10B along Prescot Road. Seen during April 1954, on the right is the Eagle & Child public house in the Art Deco style. This is a shopping centre serving the estates in the area, which is also served by many bus routes - as it is today. *H. B. Priestley, NTM*

LIVERPOOL TRAMS 1945-1957

10C LONGVIEW LANE

Liner 169 leaves Longview Lane terminus on Liverpool Road for the city as 10C on 22 August 1950. Beyond the tram stop can be seen the disused reservation to Prescot, which had closed on 26 June 1949 and been replaced by buses. The buses and trams on the 10C route took the same route into the city, and arrived at the same time, since the trams had their own reserved track as far as Old Swan. The trams on 10B and 10C were destined for Commutation Row at peak hours. *J. C. Gillham*

While the bus stop is prominent, the ornamental 'Cars Outward Stop Here' sign shares the pedestrian crossing with the Belisha beacon at Longview Lane. Here Liner 897 reaches the terminus, while 891 has reversed and stands at the neat tram shelter next to the trees, ready to return to the city centre. This view was taken on 1 June 1952, just a few weeks before closure and replacement by buses on the 21st. The trams are showing their return destination as Pier Head via Dale Street, where they will use the Centre Loop as the terminus. *J. C. Gillham*

Contrasting trams on route 10 for Prescot are seen here seen in 1948: Baby Grand 208 in the original pre-war livery with a cream roof, and 245 in the somewhat smarter post-war livery. This is the reservation along Liverpool Road beyond Longview Lane, with the modern Corporation housing estate facing the open fields, looking towards the city. The trams are travelling on the reserved track, independent of the traffic, and there is a footpath for pedestrians. *F. N. T. Lloyd Jones*

Robinson Cabin Car 800 traverses the Derby Street/Stanley Crescent loop in Prescot, with a view of the reservation from Page Moss behind it. On the Derby Street and High Street approach to Prescot there were three passing loops, and the terminus in St Helens Road was adopted for Liverpool trams after 1939. This was still St Helens tram track, but after that borough's conversion to trolley-buses in 1936 it remained in use by Liverpool trams until 26 June 1949. That conversion was brought forward to eliminate an awkward terminus in the narrow main street. *F. N. T. Lloyd Jones*

Robinson Cabin Car 807 is seen in Prescot High Street, a very narrow single-track part of the route. The tram is bound for Castle Street, Liverpool, and is followed by a Bedford lorry carrying a wartime vehicle. Sadly 807 has suffered a dent in its dash, but keeps going on the 10-mile journey. Note the bamboo pole attached to the left-hand traction pole, if needed for reaching the trolley. *F. N. T. Lloyd Jones*

Heading for Liverpool Castle Street in Prescot High Street during 1949 is famous Baby Grand 245, which happily is now preserved in Liverpool, and we eventually may see it operating on the Birkenhead new line. In the new post-war livery 245 passes the austere-looking shopping centre in the age of post-war rationing. *F.N.T. Lloyd Jones*

Bogie Streamliners 183 - still with original 'birdcage' buffers - and 979 on routes 19 and 44 respectively stand on Pier Head's South Loop in 1956. These two cars, formerly of Garston Depot until the demise of the 8 and 33 routes in 1953, are now plying their trade on the remaining Walton services. To the left is the animated scene includes several people including small boys sitting on the sea-wall, while an Austin 7 is parked nearby. If only the owner had kept it in his family, it would be worth a small fortune today! Across the river at Seacombe the Mersey cruise-boat *Royal Iris* can be seen in its distinctive livery. *Martin Jenkins*

Surrounded by hordes of buses, lone tramcar 245 on route 6A makes its way past the T. J. Hughes department store along Pembroke Place. Having climbed the slight incline up London Road and taken the right-hand fork, 6A trams gained access to Edge Lane via Pembroke Place and West Derby Street to Mount Vernon and North View. In this part of the city was to be found the 'alternative' shopping area, with such stores as Colliers, Derwent House, the Co-op, Jays and many smaller outlets, and as such was an important tram stop on the system. Happily, tram 245 is still in Liverpool today. *Martin Jenkins*

Baby Grand 237 on route 6A heads for Bowring Park at Deane Road in Edge Lane, and is about to go on the right-hand side of the dual carriageway. Note the vintage buildings on the left - now replaced by a factory - and the trees in the Botanic Gardens area, which flatter the scene in the summer of 1957. The trams will soon be finally removed from the scene in September. *Martin Jenkins*

LIVERPOOL TRAMS 1945-1957

Baby Grand 238 arrives at Bowring Park terminus on the morning of the last day's tram operation, and chalked with the sad message 'Goodbye Trams'. Looking beyond the tram - up the hill towards Broadgreen - the attractive semi-detached houses seem such a permanent feature, while the tram would be gone by the next day. Twenty years later these fine houses had been demolished to make way for the M62 motorway, and today you travel by car in a cutting at this point. *Martin Jenkins*

Just arrived at the inward tram stop at Wood Grove in Edge Lane, Baby Grand 237 looks very spruce indeed with its lower panels revarnished. In the spring of 1957 the trams were given a measure of attention to compensate for the Suez Crisis. Passengers board on a fine evening, and behind the tram the hoardings advertise the various goods of the period. To the right, on the corner of Church Road, was the garage of Crosville Motor Services. *Martin Jenkins*

The last passenger-carrying service 6A tram leaves Pier Head on the last day - 14 September 1957 - and gingerly circum-navigates the buses that will monopolise from the next day. Car 293 will travel to Bowring Park, then return to Edge Lane Depot for its preparation as 'Liverpool's Last Tram' later in the afternoon. Mostly packed with enthusiasts making their last Liverpool tram ride, it makes a very nostalgic sight. *Martin Jenkins*

LIVERPOOL TRAMS 1945-1957

On 1 September 1957 Baby Grand 213 enters Pembroke Place on route 6A to Bowring Park, and crosses the disused junction with London Road, previously used by Prescot Road route 10s. We are looking down London Road towards William Brown Street, showing the elegant traction poles and a centre bracket-pole that formerly carried the overhead frogs for the junction. There are some interesting buildings in London Road, including the Odeon on the left, and on the right an opticians, Vernon Humpage and Burton's. While the tram looks quite elegant and distinct, the road vehicles appear vintage 40 years later: a bus on route 19A, an Austin car, a lorry, an olive-green GPO van and a man on a delivery bike. Note that the tram junction was still paved in cobbles, while the rest of London Road is tarmac. *A. D. Packer*

EDGE LANE

A striking scene in Edge Lane, at Deane Road looking towards the dual carriageway, where the tram tracks are on the same side, outside the Littlewoods building. Known as the Botanic Gardens, this area shows the vintage crescent, housing firms - including Holt's fireplaces - now demolished. Streamliner 893 is on route 6A for Bowring Park, showing an advert for Vernons Football Pools and about to pass the other local pools firm - Littlewoods - in June 1954. The span wires stretch quite a distance across the dual carriageway, and elegant trees line the street. Notice the vintage gas lamp on the corner. *Richard Wiseman*

It is the teatime evening rush hour outside Edge Lane tram depot, and seven trams are lined up, bound for the city, as the local factories - including Automatic Telephone Company, Meccano and Crawfords - disgorge their workers. There is a large queue on the other side of the road, while a man passes them in his three-wheeler invalid car. Some are walking home along the pavement on this side, while others approach on their bikes and a motor bike with sidecar. The one car is trying to avoid the tram passengers! *Brian Martin*

In a fairly quiet Edge Lane, just past the depot, this is a tram rider's view of an approaching car on route 6A for Pier Head. Today this road is very busy, approaching the M62 and featuring the Edge Lane Retail Park on the right, including many supermarkets, eating places and an MGM cinema. The site on the left, where the former Crosville bus garage stood, is today occupied by several stores. *Brian Martin*

Streamliner 909 leaves the Edge Lane reservation outside Elms House, then the Youth Employment Office, in May 1955. Dating from 1918, the building was originally known as Mercia House and stood in open fields! This view shows the width of Edge Lane, and the length of the span wires that hold the street lights, while the tramway reservation has centre poles. The front window of the tram provides an excellent mobile viewing platform for the young passengers! *H. B. Priestley, NTM*

This view of the Edge Lane third track shows a newly painted 165 on an LRTA special on 4 September 1955 being passed by 6A service tram 169 and approached by 911 returning to the depot after running as a Broadgreen Hospital 'special'. Being a weekend, traffic is a lot lighter in Edge Lane. *R. B. Parr, NTM*

Edge Lane Roundabout

Left In 1951 a major event in Edge Lane was the construction of the roundabout at the junction with St Oswald's Street, where the peak-hour routes 41, 42, 47 and cross-city 48 and 49 passed. The manually operated points could therefore be eliminated and replaced by automatic points. Baby Grand 247 is rounding the tight curve, seen from a following tram that is providing a panorama across the city at this high point. The houses at the corner provide residents - including Brian Martin - with a good view of the circular! The tarmac is about to be laid over the concrete and rolled by one of Liverpool's last steam rollers - *Henry B. Miller* - in the City Engineer's fleet. *F. N. T. Lloyd Jones*

Below left A scene on Edge Lane Drive at the junction with Mill Lane in September 1946, where Standard 10 in red livery is about to reverse. The conductor has just turned the trolley, and the driver is halting the traffic while he moves the points with the iron. The indicator is showing 'OLD HAYMARKET', and the route numbers are mixed to signify a 'special'. 324 approaches on route 40, its red-on-white number indicating its terminus in South Castle Street rather than Pier Head. When route 40 was transferred to Pier Head in 1951, the route number became white-on-black, like the others there. *N. N. Forbes, NTM*

Top right A most attractive view of Standard 60 at Oak Vale on a wet day, showing the junction with Broadgreen Road and Edge Lane Drive, and the distinctive reservation of route 40. When this line was opened - 12 June 1937 - it featured street bracket arms, with scrollwork, longer than the older ones on Edge Lane. The road crossings between the reservations are marked by the small beacons. Today this scene is barely recognisable! *F. N. T. Lloyd Jones*

Middle right This nostalgic scene on 4 April 1957 shows 203 and 207 passing on the 6A route in Broadgreen Road, and a Leyland PD2 approaching bound for Edge Lane. The sharp curve in the track is reflected in the overhead, with the sinuous span-wire between the poles! The photographer is watched by a formally dressed gentleman and a puzzled-looking schoolboy. *H. B. Priestley, NTM*

Right This scene taken at Easter 1996 from exactly the same position enables the reader to compare the two scenes. In 1963 the flats were built and in 1974 the junction was blocked by the Rocket flyover - just visible beyond the footbridge. The pedestrian traffic lights indicate the position of the tram stop, and the trees have moved to the centre of the road, dividing the dual carriageway. *Steve Palmer*

This very picturesque scene on 7 April 1954 shows two Streamliners passing at the corner of Edge Lane Drive and Thomas Lane, with the local shops in the background. The scene is still the same today, with the shops, trees and playing fields, but without the trams. The plans for the 40 route in the 1930s envisaged the lines continuing from here straight up Thingwell Hall Lane and Campbell Drive towards Prescot Road, but opposition led to a diverted route when it opened in September 1937. It is clear that the grass reservation in Campbell Drive would have been ideal in the Liverpool suburban tramway tradition. *H. B. Priestley, NTM*

Here is a delightful rural setting for 167 on route 40 in Thomas Lane, with the semi-detached houses facing the playing fields and the spire of St John's Church in the distance. Opened in 1937, the tram track runs in a smooth tarmac road with the span wires from pairs of traction poles supporting the overhead and the street lights above them. Seen here in May 1955, the location is unchanged, and nearby at Knotty Ash lives comedian Ken Dodd. *H. B. Priestley, NTM*

LIVERPOOL TRAMS 1945-1957

Above A snowy setting for Baby Grand 263 as it passes St John's Parish Church, Knotty Ash, on 20 February 1955 bound for the city. This proved an ideal choice for a Christmas card by the photographer in that year! *Richard Wiseman*

Below On the same day Baby Grand 226 heads for the city on Prescot Road past Finch Lane and the junction with Brookside Avenue just down the road. There is very little traffic to be seen, two snow-covered buses are parked, and only two pedestrians in their boots! The tram tracks are clear on the reservation, without the road slush in evidence at either side. *Richard Wiseman*

LIVERPOOL TRAMS 1945-1957

6A BOWRING PARK

Left Today the site of the M62 motorway, this location is just past the Broadgreen station crossover, with 251 heading for Pier Head and the trees providing a picturesque setting. Lucas factory workers have come out for their lunch break, and are sitting by the hedge in the sunshine next to the tram stop. In June 1953, Coronation month, this was an idyllic situation! Today on the Lucas site is the Turnpike Tavern hostelry. *Richard Wiseman*

Below left The reservation grass is on fire near Bowring Park terminus in September 1955; as 169 passes workers are dealing with it, and a boy watches. The semi-detached houses, facing a country scene, were subsequently demolished to make way for the M62 motorway in a cutting. Through the grass and the hedge on the right can be seen a passing bus from Huyton. *Richard Wiseman*

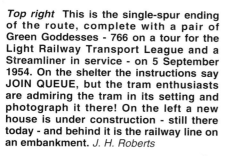

Top right This is the single-spur ending of the route, complete with a pair of Green Goddesses - 766 on a tour for the Light Railway Transport League and a Streamliner in service - on 5 September 1954. On the shelter the instructions say JOIN QUEUE, but the tram enthusiasts are admiring the tram in its setting and photograph it there! On the left a new house is under construction - still there today - and behind it is the railway line on an embankment. *J. H. Roberts*

Middle right Finally, here is a view of the original terminus in Bowring Park with Baby Grand 243 on route 6A in 1949, before the route was cut back to the central reservation on 7 February 1950. Some number indicators also had 6B and 6C, providing for an extension to Huyton that was never built. Note that the two crossovers create a loop-line allowing two trams to pass if necessary. *F. T. N. Lloyd Jones*

Right Even without the tram track, today the setting is largely unchanged, with the same trees! The fence and wall on the right and the sign for Huyton indicate the location of the M62, now cutting through the terminus. *Steve Palmer*

4A   CHILDWALL

Right The little-known 4A route to Childwall was not really part of the southern group of routes such as those to Woolton and Garston. From the Pier Head it left the city via Brownlow Hill, Wavertree Road and Picton Road as far as Picton Clock, where trams on the 4 and 4W routes turned right towards Penny Lane and the 4A continued along Childwall Road to Childwall Five Ways. But for the war it would have been extended further to the Netherley and Lee Park Estates.

Just about to ascend the slope of Brownlow Hill is Streamliner 925 on the 4A route to Childwall. The impressive Adelphi Hotel commands the scene, while the reconstruction of war-damaged Lewis's store can be seen in the background. Car 925 was one of the first to be repainted after the war in its original livery; however it has been fitted with the new girder-type buffers, replacing the old 'birdcage' type. *F. N. T. Lloyd Jones*

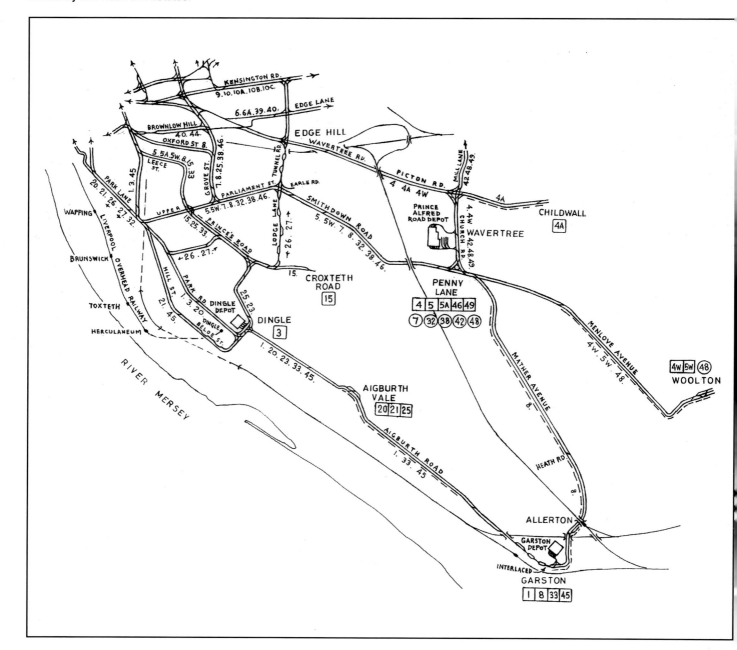

Right Childwall Five Ways was virgin territory for trams when they were extended here from Picton Clock in December 1936. Here Baby Grand car 247 is seen on the short-stub terminus in May 1948. Behind the tram is Childwall Valley Road, which would have been the route of the extension that never was. At Five Ways the shops around the roundabout still flourish, although many have changed their owners and uses since 1948! To the right - just out of the picture - is the Five Ways pub, recently refurbished with mock-Doric columns and an eye-catching landmark. Trams disappeared from here in 1949, but nothing has changed since - the reservation is still there awaiting the return of the trams! *National Tramway Museum collection*

5W WOOLTON 4W

Right Amidst the sylvan splendour of Woolton's High Street, a war-weary Baby Grand has just left the terminus bound for the city. The green open spaces of the Camp Hill estates are to be seen on the left, while behind the trees is the works of the Bear Brand Company, famous for ladies' stockings. The distinctive Liverpool-pattern street light fittings adorn the traction poles, while the track at this time is the worse for wear, giving cause for concern. Indeed this was the reason for early conversion to buses in 1949. *J. H. Roberts*

The village atmosphere of Woolton is obvious as Baby Grand 258 stands at the terminus ready for its return journey. A generous three-track layout - with three crossovers - was provided, somewhat excessive for the prevailing tram services 4W and 5W! Note the buffer stops at the end of the tracks, preventing any run-aways travelling into the then country lane of Kings Drive. On the left is Woolton Street, the shopping area, and on the right Speke Road, the preserve of buses on the 81 route. The area of the tram terminus is similar today, flanked by stone walls and used as a car park. Seen in July 1949, the trams to Woolton only had three more months to survive. *A. D. Packer*

The tree-lined and residential Menlove Avenue is the setting for Priestly Standard car 748 at the Green Lane intersection. Two boys are about to board the car, while a group of passengers on the right are waiting for a Woolton car. Today a dual carriageway road runs from Queens Drive all the way to Woolton and beyond. In these early post-war days the tram, leaving the shopping area of Penny Lane, took the left-hand points at Queens Drive and travelled along Menlove Avenue to Woolton. *N. N. Forbes, NTM*

Snow is on the ground and the bare trees await the spring as Baby Grand 275 is just about to turn from Woolton's Allerton Road into Menlove Avenue. While this is a very picturesque scene, sadly the tram is still in its dishevelled wartime state. The ancient cottages on the left-hand side of Allerton Road and the Bear Brand factory provide traffic for the trams. This particular point was the last outpost of the Liverpool tram system; beyond - as the sign indicates - was Widnes, a town that ran its own buses, but never trams. *J. H. Roberts*

LIVERPOOL TRAMS 1945-1957

46 PENNY LANE

English Electric car 764 stands on the loop at Penny Lane, awaiting its departure time on route 46, which linked Penny Lane with Walton, a cross-city route that skirted the centre of the city. From Penny Lane it travelled via Smithdown Road, Upper Parliament Street, Grove Street, Crown Street and Walton Road, which took trams on this interesting route to its terminus at Walton's Spellow Lane. The shelter in the middle of the loop achieved fame in the Beatles song 'Penny Lane', and today it is known as 'Sgt Pepper's Bistro'! *A. C. Noon*

Priestly car 748 on route 46 travels back to Penny Lane, having just travelled along Everton Road to halt at Grant Gardens. The famous and popular Hippodrome makes an imposing background. It looks like it could be a late evening, with long shadows; few people are on the tram and a lone cyclist passes a closed Boots chemist shop. To the left of the cinema is a branch of the Liverpool Savings Bank, long since swallowed up by the TSB. *Brian Martin collection*

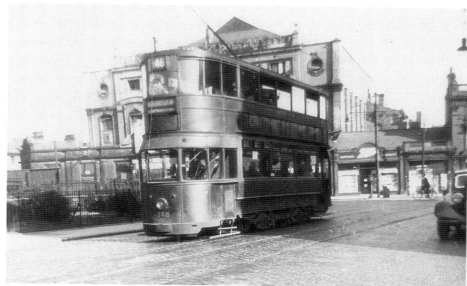

Routes 25 and 45

The 25 route formed a north-south link across the track of the inner-city, between Aigburth Vale and Walton via Prince's Road and St Domingo Road. Here two 25s, bound for Aigburth Vale, pause near Dingle Depot for a crew change. Priestly Standard 605, still with an open platform in 1947, seems well patronised on the top deck, but not one passenger inside! The second car, 724, is well filled on the lower deck and some on the platform. Note the contrast between the smaller and larger type of number blinds found on the Standard cars; 605 is seen in its later state, having started life as a double-staircase car in 1920. *N. N. Forbes, NTM*

In this picture - taken on the very last day of the tram service on route 45 - Streamliners 958 and 903 are passing in Mill Street, at Beresford Road. The short workings 45A was to Castle Street. An elderly lady prepares to cross the road, while a group of men gather on the corner. The Flemish gables of the Florence Institute for Boys is just behind the trams, and the pub - one of many in the area - was known as the Beresford Hotel, now demolished. Route 45 from the city to Garston was the 'back route' to the southern area, travelling via Great George Street, St James Street and Mill Street, gaining the main line at Dingle. The finale came on 8 September 1951. *A. S. Clayton*

Cabin Car 782 on route 25 is travelling south along Everton Road, with its inter-laced track, while in the background a tram emerges from Aubrey Street on the one-way system in Everton. In the back-ground is Village Street. On the right ladies are shopping in their headscarves, while on the left the end wall of the ter-race is being rebuilt following demolition work. Car 782 was the first of the Cabin Car series 782-817. *A. S. Clayton*

An earlier view at the Walton terminus in 1938, showing very newly repainted Robinson Cabin Car 801, with the conduc-tor replacing its trolley. Behind is Streamliner 868 on route 46, bound for Penny Lane via Smithdown Road and Netherfield Road, returning via St Domingo Road. Note the nice brick patterns on the terraced houses. *M. J. O'Connor, NTM*

LIVERPOOL TRAMS 1945-1957

St James's Church and the tower of the Anglican Cathedral are an imposing backdrop as English Electric bogie car 759 on route 3 turns into Park Road for Dingle. Streamliner 187 - on route 45 - remains on the straight tracks in Mill Street. Two members of a track repair gang stand guard by their handiwork, their red flag warning of their presence. 759 - alone in the 759-879 series - was modified and received ventilators and concealed lighting in the lower saloon only. Today St James's Church remains derelict, but is 'listed' for preservation. *N. N. Forbes, NTM*

On the way from Dingle to Walton, trams on route 3 travelled through Lime Street, where this wartime picture was taken. The imposing structure of St George's Hall, complete with its sculpted tympani - now removed - provides a background for service car 767. White-painted buffers, masked headlights and the white bollards tell us that it is 1943 and air raids are still possible. On the Quadrant, a service 24 for Seaforth stands ready for its return, while another Standard car glides from Lime Street into St John's Lane. 'Save fuel for the factories' proclaims the advertisement on the side of the 24, while a group of passengers await their trams on the island. *N. N. Forbes, NTM*

1   GARSTON

Streamliner 972 on route 1 is travelling towards the city via Park Road, and is seen passing Dingle station of the Liverpool Overhead Railway. This unique overhead railway actually reached here in a tunnel, and gave useful access to the overhead line along the docks to Seaforth. 'Through bookings to New Brighton' are available. The gentle slope up Park Road is flanked by properties long since demolished. Near the crest of the hill was the part of Dingle aptly named 'Holy Land', comprising Moses Street, Isaac Street, Jacob Street and David Street. *N. N. Forbes, NTM*

The nature of the close-knit streets of the south end of the city necessitated many peak-hour supplementary services and short workings. Here Standard Priestly car 667, showing '1A GARSTON' and well-packed with passengers, turns from Ullet Road to Aigburth Road past Toxteth Congregational Church. A Cabin Car is just about to enter Dingle Depot, and the conductor can be seen swinging the trolley. Today Dingle Depot and the Congregational Church have both been demolished. *N. N. Forbes, NTM*

Outside Dingle Depot, 781 is ready to join the peak-hour extras as a 1B to Castle Street. A bus on the former tram service 3 - converted in December 1948 - waits at its terminal stop. The tree-lined Ullet Road and Belvidere Road provide the background, while 781 still carries the *Picture Post* eyes, always guaranteed to get errant infants on board! It's drab condition emphasises its six years of wartime service with minimal maintenance. *N. N. Forbes, NTM*

Pier Head in post-war years, with 958 in the earlier livery with its crew ready to set off for Garston on route 8. We are looking at the 'A' end of the tram, and the arrow trafficators are in position, along with a triangular 'stop light'. The happy driver and conductor are looking smart in their uniforms, with the 1934-53 circular badge on their peaked hats. The driver is wearing his gloves for handling the controls, but he has removed one at the terminus to smoke his cigarette! *W. J. Haynes, Brian Martin collection*

Outside the Adelphi Hotel at Ranelagh Place, bogie Streamliner 883 approaches the junction with Brownlow Hill and Mount Pleasant, but will continue along Renshaw Street in April 1952. Until October 1949 trams on routes 8, 4A and 5 went round this curve into Mount Pleasant, but at this time only route 40 used the curve into Brownlow Hill. The framework of the new Blackler's store takes shape, while the temporary Burton's tailors occupies the frontage of the site. Along Lime Street is the newly built Palais de Luxe cinema, with its stainless steel statue of cameraman and camera. St George's Hall is visible in the distance, while on the right-hand side of Lime Street the Futurist and Scala Cinemas are flourishing. The imposing Vines Hotel, purveyors of Walker's Ales, still commands the corner of Copperas Hill. Under the Mersey Railway sign a point-duty policeman in white coat waits for the peak hour. *H. B. Priestley, NTM*

Standard car 637, on route 8 for Garston, is seen in Mount Pleasant before the closure of the line in October 1949, and the diversion of this route via Myrtle Street and Oxford Street until its closure in 1953. Outside the Shaftesbury Hotel stands a North Western bus, while a man is seen up a ladder cleaning the windows beyond the Post Office. Beyond the tram can be seen the building work of the Blackler's store on the corner of Lime Street and Ranelagh Street. *N. N. Forbes, NTM*

Trams on routes 8 and 33 diverged at the Rialto, a famous local cinema and dance-hall, which stood at the junction of Upper Parliament Street, Catherine Street and Princes Road. On the right stands the imposing St Nicholas Greek Orthodox Church, while other elegant buildings adorn the area. Streamliner 941 negotiates the intricate curved junction and turns into Catherine Street, while the track to right is only used by peak-hour route 32. The Florence Nightingale memorial still decorates the corner today. *H. B. Priestley, NTM*

Looking away from the Rialto corner into Catherine Street, two Streamliners pass over the curved junction. Both cars have undergone a post-war refurbishment, but while 937 still has the birdcage buffers, 936 has received the girder buffers and the 'via' blind 'MYRTLE ST' on route 8. The overhead wires are distinct in the picture, showing the frogs equipped with the drop-lever operated by the tram's trolley. The Georgian houses in the area have thankfully survived, and prove useful to various film companies who shoot scenes here! The cobbled sets are distinct in the picture, but with the removal of the tram tracks following its closure in 1953 a tarmac road now suffices. *H. B. Priestley, NTM*

LIVERPOOL TRAMS 1945-1957

On leaving Garston for the city on route 8, trams passed over the Liverpool Central to Warrington and Manchester line at Garston station, then ducked under the ex-LMS Liverpool-London main line at Allerton station. Seen from the latter railway bridge, the superb reserved tracks along Mather Avenue can be seen invitingly stretching into the distance. These typical Liverpool thoroughfares - designed by the former City Engineer John A. Brodie - were put in place all over the city on the new tram extensions, this one in May 1924. Together with high-class Corporation properties, Liverpool's council estates were very tasteful indeed! All built around the tram routes as a focal point, the city became accessible from all the suburbs. Here 928 heads for the city on route 8 in the early 1950s in the twilight years of the Garston circle. *J. H. Roberts*

Two Streamliners pass under the railway bridge at Allerton station; 972 is heading for the city via Mather Avenue, while 870 is an 8A, turning back at Garston and therefore not returning to the city as a 33 via Aigburth Vale. Incidentally, 870 was one of only two Streamliners to be fitted with non-Streamliner seats, having acquired 760-type seats with wooden tops. These contrast with the chrome-topped seats of 972. *Richard Wiseman*

The narrow confines of St Mary's Road at Garston forced the tram tracks into a formation of single track with passing loops and a section of interlaced track. In April 1952 Blackledges bread and cake shop stands on the corner of Sidwell Street, while opposite on Mona Street corner is the pawnbroker complete with its wares hanging outside, and three golden globes above. Behind the bus is the Liverpool Savings Bank, and dominating the street is the bulk of Garston gas works. A coal lorry turns into Church Road and a tram on route 8 enters the reserved track of Garston tram terminus. The pedestrians all seem to be dressed for inclement weather. *H. B. Priestley, NTM*

This is Aigburth Vale in the final tramway year of 1953, when only 8 and 33 routes were left to provide the service. The generous sidings and crossovers can be seen, together with the surviving trolley reverser, which at this time had no regular services reversing to make use of it. The grand shelter provides passengers with protection against the elements, and behind it is A. E. Vaughan, the well-known Liverpool wine and spirit merchant, Charles Lewis jewellers, Gillard's wallpaper shop and a pet shop. One of the Transport Department tower wagons is parked on the left behind one of the new breed of buses, and an Austin car follows a horse-drawn 'rag and bone' cart at the pedestrian crossing. A lady crosses the road with her well-dressed youngster, while another boy in school uniform watches the cameraman. The very imposing entrance to Sefton Park can be seen along the tram reservation. *H. B. Priestley, NTM*

Princes Road

Above No record of Liverpool trams would be complete without a picture of the superb tram reservation in Princes Road, which linked the Rialto and Princes Park gates. Here 928 heads for the city on route 33, about to stop for a lone passenger, while a group of boys are watching the approaching tram with great interest. Are they budding tram fans or are they waiting to use their penny returns? The tower of the Presbyterian Church of Wales dominates the fine Georgian properties along this spacious boulevard. *H. B. Priestley, NTM*

Below In April 1952 Streamliner 931 approaches the end of Princes Road reservation at Princes Park gates, and is about to negotiate the new road layout that was installed in 1950. With the demise of routes 15, 26 and 27 into Croxteth Road, the triangular junction was no longer required, so a gyratory scheme was introduced, which necessitated relocation of the outwards track. The imposing Princes Road Baptist Chapel stands at the right of the scene. The trams on route 33 took the scenic route from the city via the impressive Devonshire Road and Belvidere Road, as compared with the shop-lined Park Road. In fact, the famous Liverpudlian jazzman George Melly, in his autobiography *Scouse Mouse*, mentioned his preference for taking the 33 tram home to Aigburth. *H. B. Priestley, NTM*

Looking down the expanse of Princes Road, a city-bound 33 tram is just about to leave the well-appointed tram shelter and gain speed on the clear reserved tracks. The fine houses on this splendid thoroughfare still survive today, but many are divided into flats. The Presbyterian Church of Wales is distinguished by its spire, a landmark halfway towards the Rialto at the far end. The tracks coming off the new roundabout can be seen, and by this time - 1952 - only the 33 route trams were left to take advantage of the layout. Streamliner 874 was one of 46 trams about to be sold for further service in Glasgow following the closure of this route in June 1953. *H. B. Priestley, NTM*

The leafy lanes at Dingle are an attractive setting for Streamliner 955, as it pauses for passengers on its way from Garston to the city. The 33 route tram has turned from Aigburth Road into a short part of Ullet Road, and will then move into Belvidere Road. The track in the foreground, leading to Dingle Depot, has been tarred over and the overhead restrung just for route 33! Amongst the passengers boarding the tram are two staff from the depot, a lady in an elegant shawl and a group of schoolgirls, complete with their white ankle-socks. On the right a hand-controlled City Lighting Department cart is being pushed by one workman, while his mate gets a lift! *H. B. Priestley, NTM*

96   LIVERPOOL TRAMS 1945-1957

33 GARSTON

On the interlaced track 926 approaches the terminus in St Mary's Road, Garston, in June 1952. It may be a Sunday, as the shopping street is quiet apart from a man on his bike, a neat approaching car and family with a pram. Note the bold sign for HMV records over Smith's shop and a sign over next door shop 'BRING YOUR BOOT REPAIRS'. Streamliner 926 shows 'PIER HEAD - PRINCES PARK' on route 33, for its return journey to the city. *John H. Meredith*

Compare this scene on Easter Sunday 1996, with the Merseyside bus approaching the George public house and the surviving shops on the right-hand side, although differing in their functions today. There is a more modern store and car park on the left, changing the appearance of St Mary's Road at this point. The busy traffic has been diverted on a bypass since 1983, but the Garston bus follows the traditional route of its tramway predecessor. *Brian Martin*

The Garston circle boasted some excellent track, and none could be better than Mather Avenue, which linked Allerton Road, Penny Lane and Garston. These were Liverpool's 'Rolls-Royce' tramways, straight as a die and laid in red shale ballast enabling the Streamliners to eat up the miles at speed with ease. This was a typical 'Brodie' road layout, with grass verge pavements and dual carriageways. As shown here, at intersections and tram stops Liverpool-pattern wooden palings replaced the privet hedges. Car 928 is heading for Garston at Booker Avenue, and the tram driver has just switched off his controller to pass under the overhead line feeder. Note the de-restricted speed signs on the poles - trams certainly obeyed them along this section! *K. G. Harvie*

The lady carrying her shopping bags has just got off 926 at Allerton station, as the tram returns to Pier Head via Myrtle Street on route 8. It is about to negotiate the kink in the track to manoeuvre past the bridge abutment. The original bridge is to the right, and in the middle distance is the beginning of the reserved tracks of Mather Avenue. It was here that the original Allerton terminus was situated before the war, and the connection from here to the depot at Garston via Horrocks Avenue was only built in 1939. This link permitted services 8 and 33 on the Garston circle and a link-up between the original routes 8 and 1, necessitating 1A and 8A to signify termination at Garston. *Richard Wiseman*

Peak hours - 7 and 32

In the post-war period a number of tram services were given route numbers - like routes 7, 32 and 38 - that entailed a few early morning and late evening journeys. The 7 route was a regular service to Penny Lane, but was replaced by buses in November 1949. In this picture open-platform Priestly Standard 368, still in red and cream livery, is awaiting its peak-hour passengers bound for Penny Lane. Castle Street terminus was a useful point for peak-hour cars leaving the city via the 'back way', via Park Lane for example. In front of 368 there is a glimpse of a Streamliner displaying 'GARSTON' on its side 'via' indicator. Another Streamliner follows behind 368, still showing its pre-war advertisement for 'Tizer the appetiser'. *A. C. Noon*

Another elusive route was the 32 - again to Penny Lane via Park Lane - and here is one of Liverpool's most famous trams, long-surviving Bellamy 544, reversing on the crossover with its trolley angle-working in April 1946; the Queen Victoria monument is visible to the right. Car 544 is still in the old livery, and it survived for another three years, thus lasting ten years longer than many of its sisters! A Baby Grand can be seen in Preeson's Row, with the National Bank in James Street providing a backdrop. The pedestrians are heading towards the city office quarter - Castle Street and the Town Hall area. A roadsweeper's cart stands on the left. *Martin Jenkins collection*

LIVERPOOL TRAMS 1945-1957

BEHIND THE SCENES AND FLEET SUMMARY

Edge Lane Works

Edge Lane Works, built in 1928 on the site of the old Tournament Hall, was the most palatial tram works in the country. In the 1930s all of Liverpool's new trams were built there, and in post-war years refurbishment of trams was also carried out. In an English Renaissance style, the frontage was finished in Portland stone, while brick and steel-framed reinforced concrete provided the materials for the main shell of the building. Mock columns decorated each end of the Works frontage, while a group of offices faced Edge Lane, concealing the entrance. Surmounting all this was a fine clock tower, the finishing touch to such an eminent building. This December 1956 scene shows a Green Goddess about to enter the Works and move on to the traverser, which will take it for a ride down the centre of the huge building, and give it access to the appropriate department it requires. *R. P. Fergusson*

Contrasting with the elegant frontage of the Works, the rear was indeed very businesslike. It was entirely functional - built of pre-stressed concrete - and in May 1954 is host to a line-up of Edge Lane's surplus peak-hour cars. Prior to this time these sidings were used for trams awaiting scrapping or rebuilding in the Works, but by this time - following the closure of Green Lane Depot - Edge Lane was unable to house all its trams. Providing a contrast here is a refurbished English Electric car, seen in its last year of service. Usually the last five of these cars were stabled on the siding in front of the Works, but for some reason 766 has been separated. The chimney of the foundry is visible, and the nearest track was unwired and led to a small set of sidings where trams were scrapped in the early 1950s. It also led to a rail connection with Edge Hill railway sidings. *H. B. Priestley, NTM*

Left Two Baby Grands are being refurbished inside Edge Lane Works in 1952. In the 1930s the Works was a hive of activity constructing new cars, but these two are receiving attention to keep them running until the end of tramway operation. Car 268 will, on this visit to the works, lose its wind-up windows for a simpler sliding version, have its side indicators removed and receive a set of the smaller ventilators instead. The pre-war 'rounded' fleet numbers will also be replaced by a simple Gill Sans style. The other car has been involved in a collision, and will be rebuilt. A good supply of spare platform doors are stored nearby. *R. B. Parr, NTM*

Left This Baby Grand has just been refurbished in the Works. Its disused side indicators have been replaced by a set of four square ventilators and sliding windows, as used in buses. New panels have been fitted and it is ready for painting. The tram just visible on the right has had its side panelling removed, including its side indicators, which will be panelled over and ventilators fitted. *W. J. Wyse*

Below The intricate curvature of the Streamliners' ends posed problems when repairs were necessary. To ease these, jigs were used to pre-fabricate the end sections. Here two bogie Streamliner ends are being prepared by a bodyshop worker in post-war years. *MPTE collection*

Baby Grand 243 and sister car 242 are seen in the Works ready to re-enter service after a 1952 refurbishment. Sliding windows, Gill Sans numerals and the removal of the side indicators have transformed 243, having survived the war and austerity period with minimal attention. *W. J. Wyse*

Edge Lane Depot

The extensive site of Edge Lane Works also included a running shed at the East junction. Nine bays were provided at the front, tapering to a single track at the rear entrance, which simplified shunting movements. Here Baby Grand 274 is about to enter the front portal for the last time, having arrived as the last 40 route service car on 14 September 1957. Note the chalked legend on the side panels: 'The last 40'. *Courtesy of J. A. Peden*

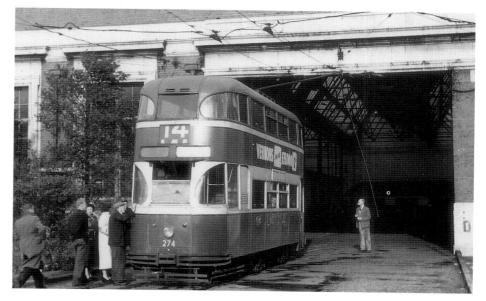

An interesting scene inside Edge Lane Depot in 1957, at a time when only the Baby Grands were shedded there. Note the ladder leading to the cleaners' gallery between the tracks, which facilitated access to the upper deck of the trams. There is also a pile of brake shoes and some sandbags on the left. The cars await their turn for service, and the crews will turn the indicators appropriate to their duty. *R. P. Fergusson*

Walton Depot

The old Carisbrooke Road horse tram depot of just four tracks was rather cramped and did not have much head-room, hence the overhead splayed to the sides. When the first batch of tram routes closed, many of the older Priestly cars were withdrawn, enabling the old Walton Depot to become a bus garage. There was also an exterior siding next to the depot shed wall, giving five storage bays in all. Of the four Priestly cars in the picture, car 581 (second from the left) has had its open platforms fitted with a pre-fabricated windscreen - note the canvas infill at waist level. This allowed the loose bodywork some flexibility over irregular track. *A. C. Noon*

Flanking the old horse car shed a new 15-track tram shed was built in 1901. Access was via Harlech Street, the other end of Carisbrooke Road, and 156 cars could be housed. Walton sheds remained in tramway operation until the last ser-vice 19 and 44 trams returned on 4 November 1956. In this scene, the impos-ing red brick and terracotta frontage is to the right, and the three access tracks can be seen. Just about to enter is Baby Grand 219, displaying 'SPELLOW LANE' on its indicator blinds, and the depot pointsman is standing by to do his duty. A bus turns into Carisbrooke Road, and in the distance is County Road, the main line for the Aintree-Walton-City tram routes. *Brian Martin*

The trams are paraded in neat lines in Walton's spacious shed. The 15 bays housed all the requirements for the Kirkby services and peak-hour routes. Some of the surviving bogie cars were shedded here with the much more economical Baby Grands. *Martin Jenkins collection*

LIVERPOOL TRAMS 1945-1957

Garston Depot

The original shed, which dated from 1910, remained virtually unchanged, and because it was set back from the roadway always remained open and draughty. When the bus garage alongside was built in 1939, three extra tram tracks were provided, making a total of eight in all. Here Maley & Taunton Streamliner 935, one of those that went to Glasgow, is seen leaving the old shed; the new extension is seen to the left, with the bus. The depot remained unchanged for many years until the closure of Garston tram routes on 6 June 1953. *J. B. McCann*

Another scene at Garston old depot, with several Maleys reposing in the sun. Car 923 is emerging on the track from the new depot building. At this time, only 8 and 33 route trams were shedded here. Today the depot is still used as a bus garage by Merseybus. *K. G. Harvie*

Litherland Depot

Providing cars for the Bootle routes - 16, 17, 18, 23, 24 and 28 - Litherland Depot fronted on to the busy Linacre Road, and shunting manoeuvres were difficult. Opened in 1903, the depot lasted in tram usage until 1950. At the end only the northern section was open, and the other three portals were closed - as seen here - for the preparatory work for the housing of buses. In the picture 278 passes on route 16 in November 1950. *N. N. Forbes, NTM*

Prince Alfred Road Depot

This depot was spacious, with front and rear entrances on Church Road and Prince Alfred Road, and contained 14 bays in the building plus four sidings outside in the grounds. The depot opened in 1928 and closed to trams in December 1949. It had much in common with Edge Lane Depot, being a through shed with access from either end. Here two Priestly Standards are seen during the last months of tram operation, showing the cleaning gallery between them. Car 368 on the left has a permanent windscreen, while 162 has been fitted with the 'pre-fab' type; Prince Alfred Road Depot fitted a number of these screens to trams, relieving the pressure on Edge Lane Works. *A. S. Clayton*

Priestly car 24, still in the red and cream livery, is seen leaving the back entrance of the depot, ready for service on the 4W route to Woolton. Immediately after the war it was realised that windscreens would have to be fitted to cars like this, and that was the reason for the cheap and nasty solution of the 'pre-fab' type; it protected the platform staff at a time when trade union pressure was being applied. *Brian Martin collection*

Dingle Depot

The original depot - on the left - dated from 1899 and housed the first electric cars, the German Ringbahns. The new extension of 1938 contrasts with the earlier ecclesiastical style of architecture, which was surmounted by mosaics proclaiming 'ELECTRIC TRAMWAYS' with a Liver Bird. Thankfully these mosaics were preserved by the MTPS when the building was demolished in 1994. Here two service cars on routes 21 and 3 pause on the siding, waiting their turn to go up to the crossover for their return to Aintree and Walton respectively. In front is one of Dingle's venerable Bellamy snowploughs, 565, unique in receiving the green livery; in 1947 all the remaining handful of Bellamys were snowploughs, except for the celebrated 544. *A. C. Noon*

Green Lane Depot

After the great Green Lane Depot fire of 7 November 1947, when 66 trams were lost, the premises were re-opened and used by trams until the West Derby Road trams on route 29 were converted to buses in April 1954. Opened in 1901, the building was demolished in 1994, 40 years after trams last used it. Standard 328 is seen emerging from the east portal; this gave access to three tracks, while the west portal gave access to another seven. Pedestrians were warned by a sign 'Beware of the Cars' on each portal. In latter days tram movements caused bottlenecks to road traffic, with the need for the trams in exit to the 'wrong' tracks as far as the Day Street crossover. *Brian Martin collection*

In this study of Green Lane's junction with Prescot Road in April 1954, one of the skeleton service 10B trams trundles over the triangular junction towards the city. The curves in the foreground were disused, the short-lived 34/35 Circular of Tuebrook/Fairfield last having used it in the 1930s. The other curves were used by regular cross-city service 49 and peak-hour 47, abandoned in 1952 and 1954 respectively. Occupying a corner of the Green Lane Depot site was the Green Lane Tavern - a Walker's hostelry - flanked by the ticket and canteen offices. In this scene zebra crossings have appeared, tarmac covered on the sets that form the infill of the tracks. *H. B. Priestley, NTM*

Edge Lane Depot sidings, seen from 'Last Tram' 293 on the final day of operation, 14 September 1957. The four tracks of the sidings are filled with trams awaiting scrapping, including two Standards that have latterly been snowploughs. Only one tram now awaits service - on route 40 - in this finale. This is an interesting view of the track layout with the left-hand curve into the Depot, and the right-hand curve into the Works. The overhead frogs have the hanging levers by which they are reset by the trolley heads - today by the last tram. *R. P. Fergusson*

Tram drivers and conductors

Above Taking a brief break for the photographer on 9 September 1956 are driver Pullman and conductor Tucker, in front of Baby Grand 266 at Pier Head. The conductor TIM (ticket issuing machine) is evident, plus his rare Liver Bird-decorated belt and buckle holding the cash bag. He subsequently became a tram conductor again in 1980 - on the Blackpool trams! *Brian Martin*

Right This is the view from the front nearside seat upstairs, from where the passengers could glance down the stairs and watch the motorman's driving skills. In this picture, taken on 230 speeding along the reserved tracks to Kirkby, the controller and the driver's stance are clearly visible, also the interlock-type controller that was fitted to the Baby Grands. Note the pressure gauges on the left, beneath the original marker lens that signified that the trafficators were lit. Just over his shoulder can be seen his right hand on the air brake lever, and under the windscreen is the conductor's red-handled emergency brake. The service timetable has been carelessly placed on the very spacious staircase. *Brian Martin*

Below Harry Tindale was a real celebrity with local tram enthusiasts, when he became the driver of the Light Railway Transport League special cars. Harry drove the LRTL 'specials' of 1954, 1955, 1956 and the very last one - 8 September 1957 - using 245. The society held two tours on English Electric car 766, one on a snowy February day and the other on a balmy September day, and he is pictured here on that latter occasion at Page Moss. An Edge Lane Depot stalwart, he served all his days on the trams until he retired in 1957, and proved that Liverpool's trams were the fastest in the country. *Brian Martin*

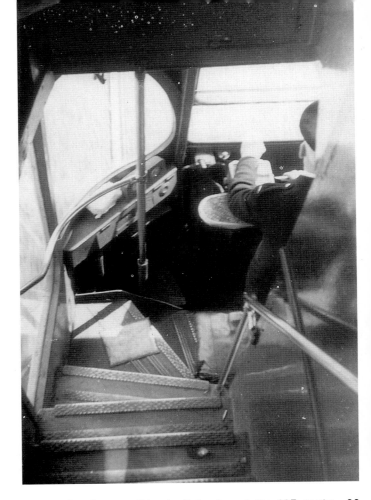

Below On the penultimate Saturday of the 10B route - 26 February 1955 - Baby Grand 267 and its crew pose for the camera at Pier Head. Driver Bob Norman, a real tram-lover and enthusiast from Old Swan, was based at Edge Lane Depot. He served as a driver until the end of tram operation, then became a floating conductor on buses. *Brian Martin*

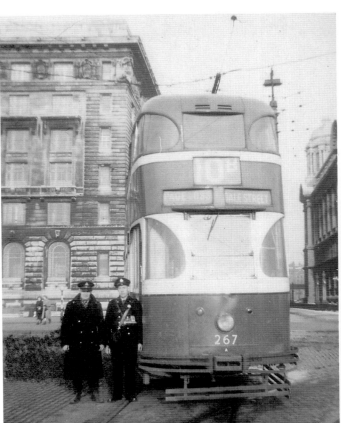

At the terminus of the 10C route at Longview Lane, the crew take the opportunity to rest during their stand time - the driver is relaxing, but the conductor seems anxious to get going! Note the shaped bakelite grab handles and the neat lamp shades on Streamliner 893. The patched seats and different seat corners indicate the 'make do and mend' attitude towards the trams at this time. The 10C route had less than a month to operate in 1952, and 897 was to be sold to Glasgow for further service. *J. C. Gillham*

Bowring Park terminus in 1952 - the driver and conductor are wearing the old 1934 circular cap badges, which the following year gave way to a simple triangular one. Tram 251 is destined for Pier Head via Church Street, while 257 is about to reverse for Edge Lane Depot. In this picturesque view the Liverpool-Manchester railway embankment is on the left, and the sylvan acres of Bowring Park on the right. Today the site is covered by the M62 motorway. *Richard Wiseman*

A final round-up of the drivers and conductors of Edge Lane Depot on 14 September 1957, to be photographed in front of 293, 'Liverpool's Last Tram'. Certainly this is a nostalgic scene, with all the crews and the Depot Superintendent George Pypes looking smart in their uniforms for the last time. After this day they would either choose to retire or transfer to the buses. *Brian Martin*

Works cars

Over the years Liverpool tramways had an assortment of stores and works vehicles, all converts from passenger cars. In this picture, seen from Edge Lane gates, 636 heads 283, 287 and 234, while behind are several Priestly cars awaiting scrap. This last generation of works cars were always found during the day parked on the south sidings of Edge Lane Works. Car 287 was ex-PW7, ex-422; 283 ex-PW6, ex-332; and 273 was former Lambeth Road-built balcony car 636, with its top deck discarded. The fourth car is the 1948-built rail-grinder 234. *J. S. Webb*

City Engineer & Surveyors Department 287 stands at the side of the Works in 1955, its two-tone grey livery getting rather tatty by that time. A group of spare cars is standing on the sidings, while a Marks bogie car has just been edged on to the scrapyard. The sheer bulk of Edge Lane Works dwarfs the trams. *Brian Martin*

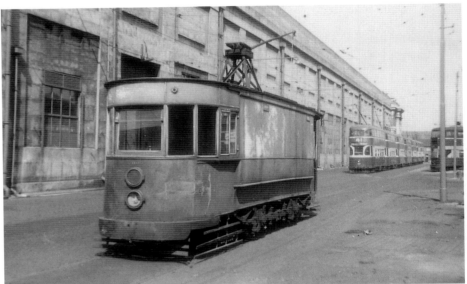

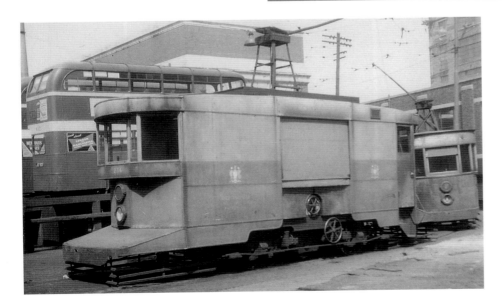

When the City Engineer's Department chose the best scrubbers and grinders remaining after the war, they surprised everyone - including the Transport Department - by constructing a new rail-grinder in 1948. After acquiring a spare truck and electrical equipment, a modern-looking vehicle emerged from the Breckside Park workshops. This tram, number 234, became the last tram to be built in Liverpool. It was fitted with motor-driven grinding equipment, which could be raised and lowered mechanically. Car 234 is seen here at Edge Lane Depot's rear entrance, and clearly shown are the handwheel controls for the grinding gear. *Brian Martin collection*

Redundant passenger cars were always given a new lease of life as snowploughs, and each depot had its heirlooms hiding at the rear. Dingle Depot's snowplough - Bellamy car 539 - is seen here in the sunlight on a rare summer venture to the front of the depot. It has canvas screens, covered-in side saloon windows and is bereft of indicator blinds. Built in 1910, it was withdrawn in 1942 after 32 years' passenger service, but became a plough for another eight years, thus serving the city for 40 years. From 1910 to 1923 it was a cream-painted First Class car! *A. D. Packer*

In 1951-52 the last of the Priestly Standard cars and the Bellamy snowploughs were being withdrawn, and the best four Standards were selected and painted all-over green. Formerly passenger cars 30, 703, 684 and 646, they were renumbered SP1, SP2, SP3 and SP4 respectively. SP1 was initially allocated to Garston, and is seen here in the depot forecourt, then went to Green Lane after the closure of Garston depot. SP2 and SP3 were based at Walton, and SP4 at Edge Lane. After the last winter of the tramway - 1956-57 - the cars were withdrawn and placed on the scrap sidings, SP1 lasting until 1958 before being cut up. *Brian Martin collection*

To capture the scene of a works car or a snowplough in action was a rare occurrence indeed. However, on a snowy Sunday morning - 20 February 1955 - SP4 was photographed on duty at Edge Lane Roundabout. Inspector Gordon Jones and a crew of three drivers and conductors on overtime salt the points on the Roundabout before heading out to Bowring Park and Page Moss to keep the tracks clear. Notice that SP4's indicators are plated over, it is in full-green livery and a two-wheeler salt-car is towed behind. *Brian Martin*

FLEET SUMMARY

400-415 Altonas
Liverpool's first electric cars were German-built, numbered in a new series to follow on from the horse cars. Motor and trailer sets were identical to those built for the Hamburg Altona tramway. Originally each motor was paired with its next number trailer, eg 400 motor and 401 trailer. Motor cars had two large arched side windows, internal division and longitudinal seating. Trailers had three unequal windows and both had 'pagoda'-type monitor roofs. Into service 1898, withdrawn by 1900.

416-429 Ringbahn
Motor and trailer sets of more conventional appearance by the same builders. Motor units had four side windows and ordinary straight clerestory roofs, trailers with three windows, otherwise similar. In service 1898, withdrawn 1900.

430-431
430 was built by Dick, Kerr in 1899 on a Curtis truck, 431 by Brill on Brill 21E truck. True origins of these two allocated numbers uncertain - information is only surmised.

432-446, 447-458
See Nos 6-20 and 21-32 respectively.

459-468
See also Nos 43-47. These ten cars were purchased from Brush in 1899 but the last five were returned as not being up to the required Liverpool specification after only a short time in service. The five remaining were purchased by Leeds in 1900 and ran in service until the late 1920s. On Peckham Cantilever trucks, they were double-deck, open-top with uncanopied platforms.

469-447, 479-484
See Nos 33-42 and 48-53 respectively.

1-4 Bellamys
Used to fill up an unexplained gap in the early fleet numbering when it was decided to number trams from 1. These four open-balcony reversed-stair Bellamy cars were identical to cars in the 484-570 series with five-window upper saloon overlapping the shorter three-window lower saloons. In service 1907, withdrawn by 1937.

5
A fleet oddity: single-ended until 1902, this open-top car was notable for its four side saloon windows and its Curtis truck. The first car to be numbered in the electric fleet (August 1900), it was fitted with a Bellamy top cover in 1905.

6-20 Philadelphias/Oceanics
Originally numbered 432-446. Single-deck centre-entrance, air-braked bogie cars by J. G. Brill of Philadelphia, supplied by Dick, Kerr in 1898. No 7 (ex-433) had one end with open sides for smokers, but was soon rebuilt. Nos 6, 8 and 20 were rebuilt at Lambeth Road into double-deckers with reversed stairs and became known as 'Oceanics'. Single-deckers withdrawn 1925/26, double-deckers 1933.

21-32
These 7.75-ton Milnes BTH cars on Peckham trucks survived longer than most early cars apart from the 'Prestons'. Never top covered or altered. In service 1899, scrapped by 1921.

33-42 Little Emmas
The first batch of Dick, Kerr 'Prestons', straight-stair uncanopied open-top cars and the most satisfactory of all the early series. Originally had headlamp on canopy but soon moved to dash. All eventually fitted with top covers, and with the series 54-133 and 141 became known as 'Little Emmas'. In service 1899, withdrawn 1921.

43-47 Westinghouses
These open-top cars were not entirely satisfactory and were never top-covered. In service 1899, withdrawn 1913.

48-53
The first electric cars built by Liverpool Corporation Tramways at Lambeth Road Works. Two side saloon windows and divided staircases were main features. Little used after the first few years and never covered. 48, 49, 50 sold in 1921 to Gateshead. In service 1899, withdrawn 1927/29.

54-133, 141 Little Emmas
Built by Dick, Kerr at Preston, these uncanopied platform open-top cars were all fitted with short top covers at Lambeth Road from 1903. In service 1899, withdrawn 1920s.

134-140
In open-top form these cars had curious square half canopies with reversed stairs of distinctive shape. In 1905 they were given Bellamy top covers but retained their odd stairs and canopies. In service 1901, withdrawn 1921/29.

142-441 Bellamys
The Liverpool 'Standard' tram built by Dick, Kerr for Liverpool Corporation Tramways was turned out in the first years of the new century at an incredibly fast rate as new tramways rapidly spread into the suburbs. Originally open-top, they were soon top covered, first by canvas blinds, eventually with glazing and

finally by the characteristically solid Bellamy roof. In service 1900, withdrawn by mid-1930s.

442-483 Bellamys
Though ostensibly a continuation of the previous batch, all cars to 471 appeared with top covers, albeit with opening roof sections and pull-down canvas blinds in the window openings. From car 472 examples were built at Lambeth Road and constructed with glazed upper saloon windows. Some cars were later fitted with extended canopies over the balcony. In service 1902, withdrawn 1936-38.

484-570 Bellamys
The archetypal Bellamy car - solid timber roof and fully glazed upper saloon extending over a shorter lower saloon. Cars in this series made up the bulk of those designated First Class cars. In service 1907, withdrawn 1937-39. Several became snowploughs from 1942 to 1950. 544 was last in passenger service until 1949.

572 Experimental Bogie
The first Liverpool car to be fully enclosed on the upper deck. An experimental prototype, it had internal stairs leading off from its centre entrance. Built by UEC on Brill 27G bogies it was the first Liverpool bogie car since the Philadelphias (6-20) of 1899. It was not an operational success, being confined to the long straight Aintree-Aigburth corridor. A series of gates and turnstiles regulated boarding and alighting. In service 1913, withdrawn 1929 after storage for several years.

573-576
These four cars spanned the transition period between the short Bellamy car with its open balconies and the extended top cover (Mallins), which afforded some protection to passenger seating outside the upper deck saloon. Reversed stairs. In service 1913, withdrawn 1938. 575 withdrawn in 1946.

571, 577-602 Double-staircase cars
Following the apparent success of the lavishly appointed prototype 571, wider and longer, with extended canopies and dual staircases at each end, a further two dozen of a similar pattern were built at Lambeth Road. However, the idea of double staircases to speed passenger flow lost momentum and the series were converted to single stairs in the early 1920s. In service 1913, withdrawn 1948-51. Originally some fitted with Peckham 8 ft 6 in radial trucks, and radial 9 ft trucks. For a period 584 and 600 were tried experimentally on bogies ex-Philadelphia cars.

603-608, 634-636 Mallins Balconies
Though the first three were wide cars possi-

bly begun as double staircase cars, trams in this small series established the adaptation of the single normal anti-clockwise spiral staircase. In service 1920-21 as simple extended open-canopy unvestibuled cars, but by the 1940s only two were left in original condition, others receiving improved modifications. Withdrawn between 1946 and 1950. 636 survived to 1954, cut down for use as s/d works car 273.

609-633 English Electric Balconies
Built by English Electric as a stop-gap due to Lambeth Road's tram-building being suspended for wartime munitions manufacture. In service in 1919, they reverted to reversed stairs and had open canopies. Only a few survived after 1938 to carry the green livery. Withdrawn between 1938 and 1948.

637-720 Standards
A large group of mid-1920s cars with enclosed upper saloons and open vestibules. Fitted with Standard Brill trucks to a whole range of long-wheelbase trucks. Latterly many were fitted with vestibules of a permanent nature while others received a more flimsy canvas and wood affair that sagged in unison with aged bodywork. In service 1924-1926, withdrawn 1947-51.

721-732 Short EMB Standards
A further batch of radial truck cars that were slightly longer (20 ft saloons). All were modernised in the late 1930s with EMB Flex trucks, vestibules and improved seats. In service 1927, withdrawn 1949-1952.

1-149 Standards
This group composed Standard trams that assumed the random numbers vacated by cars from the original series as they were withdrawn after 1921. The series also included cars from the 150-199 and 200-300 series renumbered to make way when Streamliners and Baby Grands entered service. Some of this series were little more than rebuilds and did not last long, their fleet numbers being quickly utilised again. Apart from the unique 44 built by UEC, all were built at Lambeth Road or Edge Lane between 1921 and 1931. The group ranged from open-canopy handbraked cars with longitudinal seats to fully enclosed cars with air brakes, mostly the result of extensive rebuilding and modernisation during the late 1930s. A number survived until the early 1950s. In service 1921, withdrawn 1947-52.

301-471, 572 Standards
A continuation of the previous 1-149 series split by the arrival of the Streamliners in the 150-300 series, they were displaced and renumbered mostly into vacant spaces in the 301+ group. Cars dated from 1921 to 1933 and again were a wide variety of types, a number being rebuilt from 1935 onwards

with new seats, large indicators, new trucks, motors and air brakes. Built at Lambeth Road and Edge Lane. Withdrawn 1947-52. 572 was a new Standard car built to replace the earlier experimental 572.

733-744 Standards
This series of 12 cars heralded a return to a shorter saloon (16 ft 6 in) and short-wheelbase trucks. Despite the very first fully enclosed trams 742 and 744 being in this group, not all were modified, some remaining as open vehicles, some gaining 'pre-fab' vestibules. In service 1927, withdrawn 1947-51.

745-756 Long EMB Standards
A group of long-bodied Standard cars (20 ft saloons), these cars originally had radial trucks and open platforms. Modernised in the late 1930s, all became fully enclosed and fitted with EMB Flex trucks. Nos 746 and 753 ran for a time in 1936 experimentally on Maley & Taunton bogies later destined for 941 and 942. In service 1927-28, withdrawn 1949-52.

757 'The Ghost Train'
Intended as the first of a fleet of single-deckers for use through the lower half of the Mersey Tunnel, this one short-lived experimental bogie tram was really designed for operation in pairs. However, despite its revolutionary four-axle drive through two DK120 motors, longitudinally placed to drive the axles via spiral bevel gears, it suffered operational setbacks, had cramped platforms, a narrow aisle and was prone to dewirements and derailments. In service 1929, withdrawn 1935. Built by English Electric and shares family features with the Blackpool Pantograph cars.

758-769 English Electrics
The first complete class built at the new Edge Lane Works were these fine totally enclosed bogie cars fitted originally with trucks similar to 757 concealed behind a valance. Troubles with the bogies rendered them unserviceable. Into service in 1931 in the red and cream livery, all but three (scrapped 1947) were modernised in 1937-44, repainted in green and retrucked with EMB Lightweights. Withdrawn 1953-55.

770-781 Priestly Bogies
The first cars to carry the striking new green livery of 1933, these were the original 'Green Goddesses', so called after a popular film of the period. They were fitted with EMB Heavyweight bogies developed from those used by the LCC. Originally painted with upswept cream ends, but normalised on first repaint. 778-781 were fitted with a slightly domed roof. In service 1933, withdrawn 1951-53. 773 scrapped in 1943 after war damage.

782-817 Robinson Cabin Cars
So called because they originally had an

enclosed separate cab for the motorman, these deep-domed roof cars appeared in 1933 shortly after the death of manager P. Priestly when the city electrical engineer P. J. Robinson temporarily assumed charge. They also had folding steps, platform doors and wide reversed stairs. In service 1933-34, withdrawn 1951-55. 785 scrapped after war damage 1941, 809 scrapped after serious collision 1946.

818-867 Marks Bogies
Named after the new transport manager W. G. Marks, they were not dissimilar to the Cabins, but in effect were a return to a more traditional pattern, open platforms, sliding bulkhead doors, no driver's cab and 180-degree-turn staircases. In service 1935-36, withdrawn 1951-55. 850 scrapped after collision 1945, 854 scrapped after collision 1944.

868-992 Streamliners
The ultimate in 1930s tramcar design, the Bogie Streamliners were high-capacity powerful vehicles, capable of fast speeds and specially designed for operation on the city's numerous reserved tracks. They were fitted with EMB heavyweight ('Joburg'), EMB Lightweight and Maley & Taunton Swing Link bogies. In service 1936-37, withdrawn 1953-56. Forty-six were sold to Glasgow where they ran until 1960. Several perished in the Green Lane fire of 1947. Car 869 was rescued from Glasgow for preservation and can be seen at the National Tramway Museum.

151-188 Streamliners
This series, originally intended to number 50, were a continuation of the 868-992 series. The equipment of the cancelled 12 cars was used to modernise the 758-769 series. All were fitted with EMB Lightweights except car 181, which received EMB Heavyweights. In service 1937, withdrawn 1955-56. 159, 163 and 173 succumbed in the Green Lane fire, while 171, 174 and 176 were scrapped after electrical fires in 1942, '54 and '50 respectively.

201-300 Baby Grands
An economy version of the Bogie Streamliners, these shorter-bodied four-wheelers entered service between 1937 and 1939, the last three entering service in 1940 and 1942. Embodying some recycled equipment from withdrawn Bellamy cars, they were primarily intended for street track routes. The class survived to the end of tram operation, although several were withdrawn after accidents in 1941 and 1942. Several perished in the Green Lane fire. Most withdrawn 1956-57. 293 was the last tram and is now in an American museum, while 245 was retained and is now the property of National Galleries & Museums on Merseyside and is currently in store. Fitted with EMB Flexible 9 ft hornless trucks, they were fast cars but prone to overheating problems.

UNUSUAL SCENES

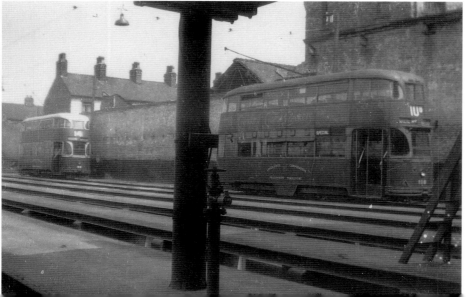

Above The Green Lane Depot fire of 7 November 1947, causing the loss of 66 trams, was famous in the history of Liverpool tramways. In the early hours of the morning, while cleaners were working on the trams, a fire started on Baby Grand 295, which spread to neighbouring trams. Since the depot was not fitted with sprinklers, the fire spread into the roof and burning wood fell on to many other trams, destroying them. The cause of the fire has been attributed to the cleaners' habit of seeking to warm the cold environment of the depot by notching the tram's controller while stationary, which created heat from the resistances. When somebody forgot to switch off 295's controller, the overheated resistances started the fire. With 10 per

LIVERPOOL TRAMS 1945-1957

cent of the fleet lost, Liverpool borrowed buses from many other operators, while Blackpool, Belfast and Manchester offered to loan trams. However, this fascinating possibility was not taken up, and the commencement of the bus conversion programme was delayed until June 1948, when tram services 26 and 27 were converted to buses.

This devastating scene shows the back of Green Lane Depot, with several Baby Grand and Streamliner cars, and the remains of the roof with ashes and water in the pits. *Martin Jenkins* collection

Below left A later view of Green Lane Depot in April 1948 with five rewired pits, now accommodating only 42 trams rather than its full capacity of 101. Comparing these Streamliners, 168 (left) has been repainted very smartly in the pre-war style, while 158 has clean new indicators but a very sooty livery! *Martin Jenkins collection*

Right A damaged Standard from the Green Lane Depot fire. *Martin Jenkins collection*

Having suffered the devastation of the Green Lane fire, when another fire started on 983 in Walton Depot at 6 am on 1 March 1954, a direct telephone line brought the fire brigade very quickly. The fire destroyed two trams and damaged ten more, while 19 trams and six buses were scorched and their windows broken. Until the overhead was brought down by the fire the staff drove trams and buses out into the neighbouring streets. Subsequently many trams were stored on the siding for football specials in Walton Lane (see page 55). This April 1954 scene shows a damaged Streamliner and a Marks car towed to Edge Lane Works for repair or disposal. *Martin Jenkins collection*

A sorry scene at Edge Lane Depot sidings on 11 November 1957 - one tram is on fire and another three have been driven out of the works for scrapping. Car 260, in the foreground, was driven on to the sidings, using a bamboo pole and cable to the trolley, and the others followed. Forty-one trams had been in stock on the last service day - 14 September - and 271 was the last tram to be scrapped, on 15 January 1958. However, two trams remained in the works, 245 and 293, scheduled for preservation. *Brian Martin*

'When men were all asleep the
   snow came flying,
In large white flakes falling on the
   city brown.'

Robert Bridges

A nostalgic look at Edge Lane reservation in December 1956, with 269 making a lonely approach towards the Roundabout, proving the point that trams were reliable in snowy weather! In the foreground the centre pole has had its stripes hidden by a spray of snow from the east. *Brian Martin*

A lunchtime scene in December 1956 in Edge Lane, with workers emerging from the factories. Trams on routes 6A and 40 are stopped at their respective shelters; the first indicates that it has been parked on the depot sidings and is covered with snow. Whereas the road is covered with slush, the trams do not have a problem on the rails, complete with sanders on their wheels. *R. P. Fergusson*

An artistic scene in Muirhead Avenue in March 1954, with a Green Goddess framed between the tree trunks leaving Almonds Green stop for the city. In the distance a tram disappears into the fog for Lower Lane terminus. *D. H. Johnson*

Above On 26 December 1956 at Edge Lane Works there is a line of trams in the snow drift, while 235 is on the Works approach line. In the foreground the depot tracks are distinct through the snow, proving that trams are in service on Boxing Day. However, the parked trams will not be needed for peak-hour specials! *Brian Martin*

Right Bellamy 502 is acting as a snowplough on the reservation at Broadgreen on 28 January 1952, with the tram stop and the trees showing the effect of the snow storm. The Bellamy car looks nostalgic in the winter scene as the plough pushes the snow off the track. We are sorry for the driver who is hiding under the reversed staircase! *Martin Jenkins collection*

Below An attractive scene in snowy weather on 20 February 1955 as Baby Grand 286 approaches the stop from Page Moss, and pleases the lady passenger waiting. Trams are perfect for safety and cleanliness in snowy weather - and do not spray slush on the waiting passengers like buses! *Richard Wiseman*

Trackwork

An interesting scene in Rice Lane in April 1938, showing the re-alignment of the track as the road is being widened. The Streamliner - on route 22 for Fazakerley - shows its striking pre-war livery and uses the track indicated by the existing span wires. In the foreground is a new nearside track with a central island, and new centre poles will have bracket arms. Compare this view with a post-war photograph of the same location on page 43. *H. B. Priestley, NTM*

This view from a service tram in Walton Hall Avenue in May 1956 shows the track gang working in the roundabout at Stopgate Lane. It is a sunny day, and the gang's jumpers are laying on the grass. The tie-bars can be seen between the rails, and repacking of the track foundation, where there was an unsteady effect on the trams, is taking place. The workers' hut can be seen level with the service trams on route 44 and the pedestrian crossing. *Alan A. Jackson*

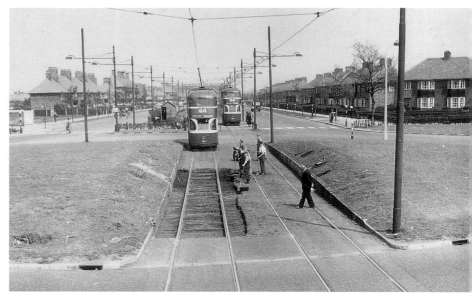

Work on the Centre Loop at Pier Head in 1955, as Streamliner 184 passes between the gang, who are resetting after track work has taken place. In the foreground the filler surrounds the new track, showing the renewal. Note that the gang all wear cloth caps and overalls, while the foreman wears a shirt with tie and waistcoat! The tram is on its way to Utting Avenue East and reminds the men about 'MACKESONS!'. *Brian Martin*

LIVERPOOL TRAMS 1945-1957

Above An accident always provided a centre of attention for the trams, since they normally conformed to normality! At William Brown Street, the Inspector tells the driver to keep on the track, while 945's front bogie has changed direction. It seems as if the Green Goddess is trying to join the bus club - which claims it has flexibility in service! *Martin Jenkins collection*

Above right The tram crew and an Inspector work on the points from Byrom Street to Great Crosshall Street, which have failed in November 1955. They have been cleaning out the dirt that has blocked the rarely used points for 902, diverted here because of a parade in the city. Note the school sign and puzzled onlooker! *D. W. K. Jones*

Clearly 219 has lost its trolley-head, and has been pushed on to the siding at Kirkby by the following 19 service tram - all the way from Southdene! The tower wagon has arrived, warning 'LINESMEN AT WORK' to refit the head. This would sometimes happen if the trolley was dewired and the head became detached by the impact on clinch-ears or frogs. The driver stands watching the linesmen, getting an unexpected break! *Martin Jenkins*

LIVERPOOL TRAMS 1945-1957

Exiled to Kirkby

After the closure of routes 19 and 44 on 4 November 1956, on the following day the 31 remaining bogie cars were driven from Edge Lane to Kirkby Trading Estate. At Delf Lane they were lined up adjacent to the railway crossing, and 153 was used as a workman's hut and a shunter. On the Monday they were swung on to the railway line - at right angles - and towed by the City of Liverpool diesel shunter for a quarter of a mile to disused sidings that had last been used by a meat packing depot during the war, and fitted the objective of keeping the trams out of the public eye.

In 1956, because of the Suez Crisis, there was a great oil scarcity, cutting the bus services, and in December the Council discussed reinstating the trams on routes 19 and 44, but voted against it. The only good news at that time was the increase of the 40 Page Moss tram service to a 10-minute headway. Sadly, the Overhead Railway was finally closed on 30 December, and the trams at Kirkby were scrapped by April 1957; the Streamliners were lost for ever, although some were at large in Glasgow! *Brian Martin*

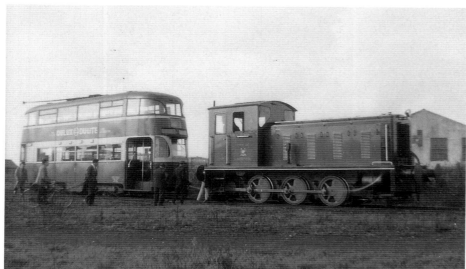

'Down With Hall' is chalked on the dash panel of 992, expressing the sentiments of the locals at this scene of 31 Streamliners on the remote sidings at Kirkby, exiled from their native tramway in the city. *Brian Martin*

LIVERPOOL TRAMS 1945-1957

Last nights, 1956-57

Right 'LAST 19' and 'END OF KIRKBY' are chalked on the panels of 206 as it is about to return to Walton Depot from Kirkby for the last time on 3 November 1956. As the tram stands at the lonely location of the Boundary Road reservation, the enthusiasts and its crew pose - a nostalgic scene! *Martin Jenkins*

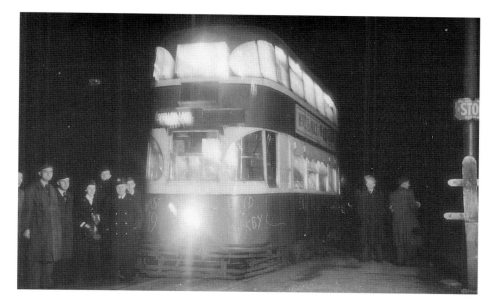

Below The surviving Baby Grand 245 and its crew pose for its last journey from Bowring Park on the final night, 13 September 1957. *Martin Jenkins*

Above Baby Grand 238 was the last 40 from Pier Head to Page Moss at 9 pm on the last night. Later service 40 trams turned at Pilch Lane and returned to the depot. *Martin Jenkins*

Left During the last week of tramway operation, 293 operated on routes 6A and 40, and is seen at Bowring Park one evening in this historic guise. *Martin Jenkins*

FINALE:
LIVERPOOL'S LAST TRAM

IT WAS HARD to believe that 14 September 1957 was the last time that we would see Green Goddess trams in Liverpool. Twenty-six trams were in service in the morning, 14 on the 6A and 12 on the 40. However, after the morning peak period buses replaced trams using the tram stops. The last 6A was 293 at 1.53 from Pier Head, departing Bowring Park for Edge Lane Depot at 2.36. The last tram in service was 274 on route 40, which left Pier Head at 3.58 and departed Page Moss at 4.40 for Edge Lane. That was the end of tramway services in Liverpool.

We arrived at Pier Head under greying skies that morning, and took photographs of the service trams that we were pleased to see frequently. Great was the consternation of the tram enthusiasts when the first bus on route 6A arrived, and gradually the trams became rare, having slogans like 'Goodbye Trams' and 'Last Day' chalked on their sides. We realised that the end was near, and it was a thrill when the repainted cream and green 'Last Tram' 293 arrived - in service! We boarded for a nostalgic service ride to Bowring Park on a historic tram! Its appearance was certainly striking - during the final week some locals thought it was a new tram!

Top left **Pier Head on the last morning with 274, which was to be the final departure in service, and the crew from a replacing bus on the 6A.** *Steve Palmer*

Middle left **Another scene at Pier Head on the final morning, with 6A and 40 trams, the River Mersey and the landing stage for ferries. Car 245 looks smart, having been selected for preservation.** *R. P. Fergusson*

Left **'Last Tram' 293 arrives in service - a large queue is waiting at the tram stop for a reminiscent ride!** *R. P. Fergusson*

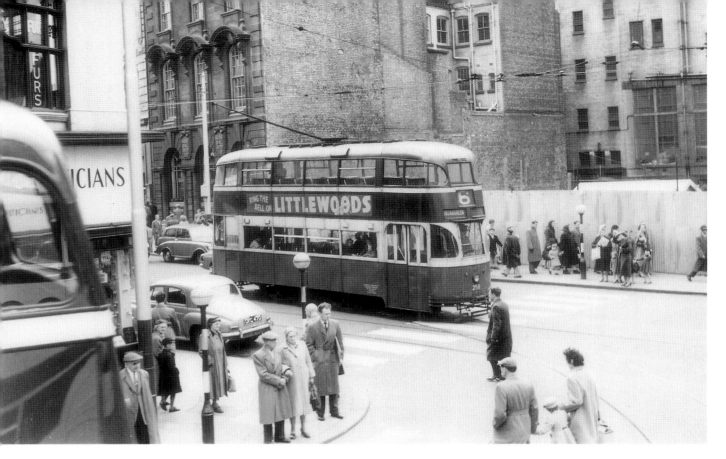

Above A view from the 'Last Tram' in service, as people in the streets proudly stare as it passes - its reflection can be seen in the side of the new bus alongside. We are being followed by 258 on route 6 to Broadgreen, one of the last trams to turn there. *R. P. Fergusson*

Below The scene at Bowring Park at 12.15 pm on the final day, as the driver turns the trolley of 293, which is the centre of attention. It is followed by 237, which shows blank indicators and will return to Edge Lane Depot, while the replacing bus takes over its duty. *R. P. Fergusson*

The final 6A and 40

On its last service journey on route 6A, and fully loaded, 293 is seen from a replacing bus in London Road, reflecting its profile in the wet street surface. At Bowring Park a crowd was beginning to gather, as the last service tram was to leave at 2.36 for Edge Lane Depot. *M. Harrison*

When 293 arrived at Edge Lane, all the passengers had to get off before it went into the depot for cleaning, ready for the evening finale. Here the tram - and the author - is captured in the doorway. *M. Harrison*

A historic view at Pier Head, as the last service tram, 274, departs for Page Moss, through the lines of buses in front of the Mersey Dock & Harbour Board building. Before its departure from the stop, a large queue had formed to ride on the tram. When it was packed to capacity, four Inspectors arrived, one blew a whistle to signal departure and another mounted a ladder and covered the tram stop with a black hood. The tram service had ended for ever! *Steve Palmer*

The procession at Pier Head

Right A sensation was created at 5.35 pm when the decorated 210 arrived at Pier Head, leading the procession of 13 trams for the finale. A crowd had gathered, and many rushed forward to take 210's picture, as seen here. The official LCPT band started to play, adding to the memorable occasion. *R. P. Fergusson*

Below The service buses had departed from Pier Head, allowing the trams their last correct place on the South Loop and approach track. The 13 trams were lettered so as to be identified by their ticket-holders, and they all showed '6A BOWRING PARK - PRIVATE' on their indicators. This made a final familiar sight at Pier Head. *M. Harrison*

A close-up of 226 and 245 - lettered 'H' and 'C' respectively - looking very clean in the evening sun as they fill with passengers. Cars 210, 264, 214, 235, 213, 226, 266, 260, 296 and 252 are filled with ticket holding passengers, while 245 and 207 carry retired LCPT staff, and 293 conveys the dignitaries. *Steve Palmer*

This is the view from 213 - car 'J' - showing the crowd surrounding 293, as important guests arrive, including the Lord Mayor and MP Bessie Braddock. When the Liver Building's clock chimed 6 pm, the band struck up 'Wish Me Luck As You Wave Me Goodbye' and all the ships in the river sounded their horns. All the trams then left in convoy, round the loop, with Pier Head echoing to the resounding serenade! *Steve Palmer*

The 'Last Tram' leaving Pier Head, escorted by police motor cyclists and surrounded by buses that sound their horns in salute. The buses have finally triumphed over the trams! Certainly 293's livery enhances its appearance. The ladies in the crowd are waving to the famous passengers. *J. A. Peden*

LIVERPOOL TRAMS 1945-1957

'Liverpool's Last Tram'

The procession of trams moved through the city centre at funeral pace, and when they turned into Lime Street with decorated 210 at the front, they once more dominated the whole street. Once they reached the reservation, they accelerated a little, and there were crowds at each stop, some with boys on the shelter roof! At Bowring Park a huge crowd has assembled, seen here from 252 ('D'), as 245 has its trolley turned and 207 and 293 wait. Two boys are having their picture taken in front of the last tram, and a boy on his bike follows. *M. Harrison*

At Edge Lane a huge crowd is seen as we approach, and as the trams stop we join them. Each tram swings through the police cordon at the gate into the depot, then finally 293 appears solo, and without stopping is seen leaving Edge Lane for ever. The crowd waves to the dignitaries and cheers, while the police join arms to keep the crowd outside. *R. P. Fergusson*

This scene of the 'Last Tram' halted on the curve was taken over the heads of the crowd, and shows the police watching but two boys unable to see! The band strikes up 'Auld Lang Syne' as 293 moves slowly across the front of the works to disappear finally through the doorway - for ever! *Steve Palmer*

=THE OUTCOME, AND SURVIVALS=

A new life in Glasgow

With the demise of the Garston circle in June 1953, LCPT advertised its surplus trams for sale to the remaining undertakings still operating them. Glasgow took up the option and initially purchased the 24 Maley & Taunton Streamliners displaced from Garston. The bargain price of £500 each was only part of the cost, as Glasgow spent a further £2,400 per car for service in that city. The body of 938 is seen on the specially constructed transporter in Old Swan, on the weekly Saturday morning trip. The bogies were transported separately. *Brian Martin*

In Glasgow, some of the ex-Liverpool cars were temporarily stored at Newlands Depot, seen here being shunted by the Standards. Liverpool's 871 is one of the second batch of 22 cars sold in April 1954, this time for £580. These were cars displaced by the closure of Liverpool's 29 route. By coincidence, in Glasgow these refurbished cars were utilised on that city's 29 route. Great play was made by the Liverpool Transport Development Association, who distributed protest leaflets - 'Route 29 - but not in Liverpool' - depicting one of the resplendent ex-Liverpool cars in use in Glasgow. *Richard Wiseman*

The first car to enter service in Glasgow was ex-Liverpool 934, numbered 1007 in its new home. Since these cars had rounded ends and were longer, the buffers were removed, and bow-collectors were fitted, which made them faster still! Service 29 was a 12-mile journey from Milngavie in the north to Broomhouse in the south, where 1007 is seen. At first the ex-Liverpool cars were seemingly a good buy for the city of Glasgow, which wanted to retain the major trunk routes operated by modern cars. However, problems soon developed, water ingress became a major nuisance and modifications were made by installing one-piece windscreens. *Richard Wiseman*

LIVERPOOL TRAMS 1945-1957

Central station, Glasgow, is a famous location to capture this view of 1014 on service 15 - Anderston Cross to Bailieston - passing a Coronation 1276 on 5 September 1959. I waited for this picture by the 'Hielandman's Umbrella', which was part of Argyle Street and contained permanently lit shops. Hope Street is to the left, where route 29 cars would appear from Milngavie. By this time the former Liverpool cars had acquired a small port-hole window on the front of the upper saloon, to ease bow-collector change-over, and Glasgow-type trafficators. *Steve Palmer*

Left The demise of the Liverpool cars came with the eventual contraction of the Glasgow system from 1956, and by March 1960 there were only seven still running. On 21 February of that year a farewell tour was held on one of the remaining cars, 1055 - ex-Liverpool 869 - when it toured many parts of the city, some 'foreign' to this type of car. The tour was organised by the Liverpool University Public Transport Society, and it was on this tour that the idea of preserving the car was germinated. The sponsors collected £50, aimed to act as a deposit to save the car from scrap. The tram is the centre of photographic attention in this lovely scene in the snow on Mosspark Boulevard. *M. Harrison*

Below Car 1055 (869) is seen again at Auchenshuggle, in company with the Cunarders and a Standard, on the tour. The dark-coloured lining round the indicator boxes shows that sticky tape has been applied to resist water leaking in. This partly worked, but left the cars looking decidedly unkempt and shabby. *M. Harrison*

869 restored

After the success of the Glasgow tour with the former 869, moves were made by LUPTS - with the help of local tram enthusiasts - to secure the tram for preservation. It was taken to the Middleton Railway in Leeds, where there were plans for a running tram museum, although this did not materialise. Here 1055 has just been delivered to Parkhurst sidings in Leeds, but the 4 ft 7¾ in Glasgow gauge made the car incompatible with the standard gauge sidings at 4 ft 8½ in. As a result a four-wheel truck had to be used, and after the collapse of the Middleton Museum plan 869 was taken to the National Tramway Museum at Crich in Derbyshire. *Brian Martin collection*

After five years at Crich, stored in the open, it was clear that progress was disappointing. However, with the help of Liverpool Transport and the Merseyside Civic Society, space was allocated in the former Green Lane tram depot, and 869 was brought back to Liverpool in 1967. Here 869 has just been delivered to Green Lane Depot and jacked up ready for the long restoration to begin. It took the MTPS 12 years of fund-raising and hard work to be able to send 869 back to Crich in 1979. Its pristine condition - resplendent once more in its Liverpool green and ivory - raised anticipation for rides on a Green Goddess again. *D. Webster*

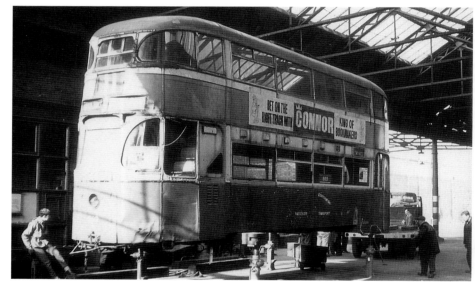

On reaching Crich in 1979, local enthusiasts were disappointed that the car could not immediately enter service, but unfortunately serious truck fractures precluded its use. It was another 13 years before funds became available for this engineering work to be completed. Eventually, 869 ventured out of the workshop under its own power on Sunday 20 December 1992, and went into passenger service following an exhilarating visit by MTPS members in July. The workshop staff were presented with a Liver Bird, and 869 proved to be one of the most popular trams in the large museum collection. Here 869 is pictured at the Glory Mine terminus of the Crich tramway during the MTPS visit. *Brian Martin*

LIVERPOOL TRAMS 1945-1957

Baby Grands
245 and 293

Baby Grand 245 had the honour of being used on the final LRTL Liverpool tour on 8 September 1957, and was retained after all the other trams were scrapped. It was stored in the paintshops at Edge Lane Works until spruced up to grace the 1973 Liverpool Show; the LCPT stand had never previously displayed a tram along with its latest buses. Car 245 is seen here - not quite sitting on the surviving rails at Edge Lane Works - awaiting its low-loader for transportation to the show. In 1977 the Liverpool Museum - not able to exhibit the car in the transport gallery - loaned 245 to the Steamport Museum at Southport. Unfortunately some deterioration occurred until it was brought back for exhibition in the Princes Dock large objects collection. When that closed for redevelopment in 1992, 245 was hidden in private storage in Bootle - but one day it will emerge to be seen and ridden upon by the public. *B. Taylor*

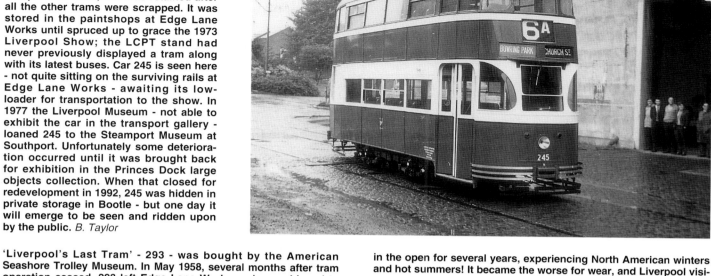

'Liverpool's Last Tram' - 293 - was bought by the American Seashore Trolley Museum. In May 1958, several months after tram operation ceased, 293 left Edge Lane Works and was shipped to Boston USA, for onward transport to Kennebunkport in Maine, where it joined trams from all over the world. Unfortunately it stood in the open for several years, experiencing North American winters and hot summers! It became the worse for wear, and Liverpool visitors to the Trolley Museum were disappointed at its poor condition. However, attempts to bring it back to Liverpool have been rebuffed by the American Museum. *Martin Jenkins collection*

Wirral Heritage Tramway, Birkenhead

To ride on a tram in Merseyside these days, you have to go to Birkenhead home of the Wirral Heritage Tramway, seen here on Easter Sunday 1996. Outside the restored Pacific Warehouse, No 70 is having its trolley turned, while the public are waiting to board. To operate the new Heritage Tramway between Woodside Ferry and Pacific Road, Wirral Council purchased two newly built trams from Hong Kong Tramways - for £85,000 each - and had them finished in the original Birkenhead livery of dark maroon and cream. They were given the numbers 69 and 70, following the highest Birkenhead tram fleet number of 68. *Steve Palmer*

The scene inside the museum - featuring working trams Birkenhead 20 and 69 on the wired track in the centre, and the MTPS compound allowing the public to inspect a display and restored trams, including horse tram 43 and English Electric 762. This is one of the celebrated survivors from the Liverpool fleet, which was withdrawn and cut down to become Newsham Park bowling shelter in 1955, and rescued by the MTPS in 1977. The upper deck and platforms were rebuilt by the society and fitted to the original body. A world-wide search for its EMB lightweight bogies was unfruitful, so a pair of EE bogies was acquired from Blackpool, formerly used on Balloon 705. *Steve Palmer*

Birkenhead 20 - a beautifully restored tram - is seen on the Heritage Tramway in 1996. The MTPS, after using Green Lane Depot as a workshop, spent time at Speke Airport and the large objects store at Princes Dock. It was then allocated space at Pacific Road sheds on the Wirral Heritage Tramway. It was fitting that Birkenhead 20 - an open-top four-wheeler dating from 1901 - should be completed in its native town. The car has been track tested - as seen here - and is at present awaiting official sanction for operation. Certainly this will give the public great enjoyment. *R. S. Jones*

LIVERPOOL TRAMS 1945-1957

Right At Easter 1996, only the first phase of the tramway is open, but a new extension from Pacific Road depot along Shore Road to Egerton Bridge opened in July. Blackpool Transport Services have operated the service cars on the line on behalf of the Wirral Council since commencement in 1994. Here Birkenhead 70 is seen on its test run, about to turn into the terminal stub, with the tower of Hamilton Square station of the Merseyrail system in the background. A further extension to this location is under consideration.
M. Mercer

Below Stop press. . .

DAILY POST

NORTH WEST NEWSPAPER OF THE YEAR — Daily PAPER OF THE YEAR

Thursday, September 22 1994 — Weather: Misty start, sunshine later — Price 30p

LOOKING FOR WORK?
PAGES OF JOB VACANCIES START PAGE 17

SCALES TIPS IT O
See Back Page

RETURN OF THE TRAMS
£75m plan for new Merseyside rail link

2am LATEST

Leather works up in flames
By Richard Elias and Eric Langton

A HUGE blaze engulfed British Leather's Birkenhead works early today.

Fire crews manning 13 appliances were fighting the flames leaping from the roof of the 50ft high building and there were some reports of explosions.

New Chester Road was blocked off as the walls threatened to collapse and police say it may stay closed for some time.

Taxi driver Derek Smith said: "It is blazing. The building is going to be absolutely destroyed."

At its height 20 fire appliances and three turn-table ladders were in
● Continued on Page 2

By Mark Currie Daily Post Staff

A LIGHT rail transport system could be carrying passengers around Liverpool within three years.

The return of a modern, rapid version of the tram was unveiled by a private-sector consortium yesterday.

The Liverpool Light Rail Group says the £75m light-rail service, linking south Liverpool with the city centre, could be the first of six routes operating on Merseyside.

Agreement

The consortium, involving electricity generator Powergen and bus companies Merseybus and North Western Roadcar, revealed its plan to members of the Liverpool Chamber of Commerce and Industry.

Consortium spokesman Lewis Lesley, professor of transport science at John Moores University, said, the first scheme could create 120 jobs, with a further 500 during construction and 600 jobs created indirectly.

Mr Lewis explained it plans to run the service from Speke, with a spur to Liverpool Airport, and into the city via Speke Hall Avenue, Mather Avenue and Smithdown Road. Subject to agreement with the city council, the route would loop around in
● Continued on Page 5

2001 SET FOR TRAM ODYSSEY
By Delian Johnson

DETAILS of plans for a new multi-million pound tram scheme for Merseyside were unveiled today . . . .

Public voice on tramway
By David Charters

PEOPLE are being given the chance to say whether Liverpudlians should ride into

Plans revealed for Mersey's transport scheme

Trams to Page Moss?

MERSEYTRAVEL'S vision of trams of the future has taken to the road — making sure everyone has their say.

The exhibition is being staged at public libraries along the proposed first route, which would link Page Moss with Liverpool City Centre.

It was chosen for its high patronage potential — and because it is unserved by the extensive Merseyrail network.

But Merseytravel has stressed that the . . . . . informative stages —

By Neil Roberts Daily Post Staff

TRAMS could return to Merseyside as planners behind two futuristic transport schemes start working together.

Merseytravel and a consortium called the Liverpool Light Rail Group are working on two different projects to bring trams — or 'guided buses' — back to the banks of the Mersey.

And now officials representing the two groups have started regular meetings to discuss combining their ideas into one overall rapid transit project for Merseyside.

The Government has already said it will only fund one tram scheme for the area.

And the total cost of the

the ambitious project — costing between £60m and £100m — might look like.

Three types of technology are under scrutiny — and Merseytravel's Chair Mark Dowd said the consultation process would take full account of community views and opinions.

'This would be a massive commitment to make. Before we choose technologies or look at funding, we must ensure the wishes of the people are taken into account,' said Councillor Dowd.

The exhibition opened on November 16 then Kensington

Trams on way back

£150m project planned to start in 2001

Tramlines across Merseyside

Liverpool Light Rail Group

Trams are already running

£75m light rail system unveiled as transport of the future from Speke to city centre

Trams may roll again

AN ULTRA-MODERN version of the popular trams could be running in south Liverpool within three years.

The plans for a £75m light rail system in the city have been unveiled by the Liverpool Light Rail Group, a private sector consortium, involving Powergen, Merseybus and North Western Roadcar.

They have completed the groundwork for a light rail project linking Speke, including the airport, and Garston with the city centre.

Encourage

Consortium spokesman Lewis Lesley, professor of transport science at the city's Sir John Moores University, said the city centre-Speke line would be the first of six possible light rail links across Merseyside. It would create 120 permanent jobs, with 500 others during construction. The service will run from

Speke, with a spur to Liverpool Airport, and into the city along Speke Hall Road, Mather Avenue and Smithdown Road.

The aim would be to encourage more private car users off the roads, particularly at peak times.

"We believe what we are proposing is essentially a free light railway line which will supplement existing traffic and transport policy in the city. The target is to open in 1997," said Prof. Lesley.

The consortium has submitted a bid for £15m over three years for Objective One cash to take the project off the drawing board.

Merseytravel chief planning officer Brian Knowles welcomed the proposals.

He said: "We are very interested in this development which would be a great improvement in public transport provision on Merseyside and we will be looking to support it."

Rail system project

The light rail transport system is planned to run from Speke, with a spur to Liverpool airport, and into the city via Speke Hall Avenue, Mather Avenue and Smithdown Road.

Target: to open in 1997, 40 years after the last tram ran in Liverpool

Smithdown Road

Mather Avenue

Speke Hall Avenue

City centre

Speke

Getting Liverpool moving

River Mersey
Liverpool City Centre
Albert Dock
Allerton
Wirral
Garston
Speke
Liverpool Airport

with Light Rail Transport.

INDEX